God Does Love Me

My Trans Journey
To Finding My True Self

By Dawn J. Flynn

Copyright © 2012. All Rights Reserved

Dedication

This book is dedicated to my Creator, God and Savior for His love, grace, and acceptance that allowed me to embrace who I truly am.

To my Mom and Daddy for the love they gave me and the faith they instilled in me that brought me back from the throngs of death to a new and better life.

To my dear friend and coworker, Carrie, who was the first person I told that I was transgendered. Her acceptance and love gave me the courage to pursue my dream.

To my therapist, Dr. Lisa Griffin, who saved my life by showing me that in being transgendered I was just being my true self.

To my soul mate, Pam, who is, and always will be, the love of my life.

Table of Contents

Forward	7
Preface	9
Introduction	11
Chapter 1: **Discovery**	15
Chapter 2: **School Dreams**	29
Chapter 3: **Losing Myself in Alcohol**	53
Chapter 4: **Be a Man—The First Try**	65
Chapter 5: **Be a Man—The Second Try**	99
Chapter 6: **The Pageantry of it All**	139
Chapter 7: **Rejected Ministry**	157
Chapter 8: **Finding My True Self**	175
Chapter 9: **Becoming a Woman**	183
Chapter 10: **The Final Step**	217
Chapter 11: **Life With Joy**	229
Acknowledgements	239
About the Author	241

Forward

As a boy, Duane was obedient, and he played it safe. He became a scientist, a husband, a father, and a Methodist minister. Who could find fault in all of those good and wonderful things? To the world, Duane was a good man. But, no one's life is perfect, and only God knew how deeply unhappy he truly was. Only God could say, 'it's okay to be...'

Luckily, or not, depending on your outlook in life, at some point in the lives of believers, God speaks to each of us. 'He' gives us a sign, or sends a message. Our responses to God's little nudges are as varied and extreme as we are. Some, out of fear, tradition, or self-sacrifice will ignore the signs. Others will choose to hear only part of the message and make what they think are appropriate modifications. A few brave souls will receive what God is showing them and actually attempt to step wholeheartedly into what God has planned for them; but for reasons only God truly knows, stop just short of full surrender. Fewer still will have the faith it takes to truly ask for God's guidance, stop and listen to the answer, and then risk losing everything they've been 'given' to be the person their God told them to be. Few people will ever be tested in such a way. Fewer still will be as bold as Dawn Jennifer Flynn, who, on her journey to find PEACE, armed only with FAITH that surpasses all understanding, risked losing everything that the world said was 'good'... just to BE.

T. Randall Jones

Preface

The whole idea of writing a book is amazing to me. I have been an avid reader my whole life and have the utmost respect for those gifted writers who so eloquently express ideas and thoughts in ways that make your heart move. I never considered myself a member of that select fraternity (or sorority).

Yet, here I am. Why you ask am I writing now? The reason is that recently I have learned that when one has been blessed and fortunate to experience life in a grand scale, one has to share it. Not only have I experienced life in a grand scale, but I have experienced it from both sides. Let me explain.

I have been blessed to live my life in both genders. As the title of this book suggests, this book is about my transgender journey to find my true self. Let it be known from the start, I do not, in any way, feel my life in the male gender was without value. Everything we experience in life is a teaching tool. And now that I have found my true self, I am able to see life through unique lenses. In fact, now I don't just see life through my eyes. Now I see life with all my senses and that makes life worth so much more.

I have also been encouraged by many friends, both transgendered and natal, to write down my journey as it includes so many unique experiences. They feel that the lessons I learned can possibly be helpful to someone else who is struggling with similar issues about their gender identity.

If my story does help someone in any small way to better understand who they are and know that God loves them just as they are, then this book has done well. My wish is that wherever your journey takes you in life, you will go with joy in your heart and know within your soul that you are truly on the journey you were meant to be on.

Dawn J. Flynn
Gastonia, NC
June 2012

Introduction

My childhood was like most other boys during the 1950's and 1960's (i.e. school, playing marbles, playing catch, playing tag football, collecting baseball cards) except I was thin (most other boys were more stocky) and I had softer features than they did (i.e. my face wasn't chiseled as most boys). Many of my friends and my Mom and Daddy's friends noticed. They didn't make fun of me but I remember comments like, "My, he's sure a pretty boy", and "He needs to put on some weight if he's going to play football someday". Because I was the only child to survive Mom's pregnancies and she was very protective of me, I wasn't allowed to play sports.

Mom was afraid that her only child would get hurt because in the back of her mind she knew she would never be able to have any more children. Later I was bullied in school for my soft features and not being able to play sports with my friends. I didn't understand why I couldn't join the other boys. Mom's argument didn't make sense to me. I would be careful not to get hurt. My friends hardly ever got hurt playing sports. Didn't she know that forbidding me to go out for sports was making me get bullied? I started asking myself questions like: "Why were my features soft and not like other boys?" "Was there something wrong with me?" and "If I wasn't allowed to do 'boy things', was I really a girl?".

This is when my early sexual identity conflicts started to appear. I started to do things that were traditionally identified with being a girl like avoiding rough and tumble play. I had boy friends at home that

I played with (cowboys and Indians, baseball, and touch football) but I really liked playing with the girls more. They were nicer and I secretly admired their dresses and that they could play with dolls. For as long as I can remember, I always wanted a Barbie doll. But as a boy of course I couldn't say anything (When I told a girlfriend during my transition that I had always wanted a Barbie doll she was touched and bought me my first Barbie. I was thrilled!). Because I was a boy I had to be satisfied playing with guns when I really wanted to play with dolls.

One of the most dramatic events of my childhood happened during a visit to my paternal grandmother's house when I was 8 years old. I loved my grandmother so much. She was a great cook and made cherry pie for me, my favorite, when I came to visit and on my birthday.

She was a large woman and jovial all the time. Growing up I remember thinking that Mrs. Santa Claus must be like her. So, I would ask Mom and Daddy to take me to see her as often as possible. During one of those visits, while Grandma was in the kitchen cooking, I started doing what most 8 year old boys do – I ran through the house! It was great fun as I was investigating different rooms in the house. When I came to her bedroom I noticed the door was open. It was never open. She usually had the door shut. "Oh boy", I thought. "This will be fun". When I looked inside I was amazed.

First thing I noticed on the right was that her closet door was open. Hanging on the back of the closet door was a huge front snap corset/bra. I looked at it in amazement wondering how she was able to stand having it on all day. I remember thinking how uncomfortable it must be for a woman to have to wear corsets and bras. They were so restrictive. Then I turned to the left and faced her dresser mirror which was attached to the back of her dresser. There, on her dresser, I saw something that grabbed my attention – the prettiest pair of pink pearl clip-on earrings.

I stared at them for a few seconds in amazement. I knew that Mom wore earrings and I had always thought they were cool but here in front of me was a pair that I could touch! I just couldn't touch Mom's earrings. I carefully picked them up and held them up to my ears while looking in the mirror. Then a life changing thought entered my mind – "Why don't you put them on? No one would know." I stood there and argued with myself that boys are not supposed to want to wear earrings. I looked at them again with admiring eyes for they were so pretty. I lost the argument. I rationalized that I was only playing and it was okay. With shaking hands, I pulled the clip back on one of the earrings and put it on.

I looked in the mirror and was mesmerized. Shaking even more, I pulled the clip back and put the second one on the other ear. Then I stood, looking in the mirror at what used to be a boy. But instead now I saw a girl looking back and amazingly I liked it. I liked it! I don't know how long I kept the earrings on and admired myself in the mirror but I left them on as long as I could.

Eventually Grandma called my name and I had to take them off. I pulled them off and carefully placed the earrings back on the dresser where I had picked them up. But when I pulled them off, I started to cry. I cried because I didn't want to take them off. They felt right when I had them on. I knew deep down that a boy shouldn't feel this way but I did.

From that day on, I knew I was different. I knew I had feelings that boys shouldn't. I also knew that I couldn't tell Grandma, Mom, Daddy, or anyone. No, I definitely couldn't tell anyone. I had to keep this my secret until I could figure it out.

Chapter 1

Discovery

Mom had a hard life before she met Daddy and this hard beginning not only had a great bearing on Daddy's willingness to accommodate her requests, but on my story as well. Mom was born Helen Elizabeth Ostrander on June 29, 1927 in Detroit, Michigan and grew up during the Great Depression on a farm in the Upper Peninsula in Michigan outside the town of Whitefish.

Mom's parents, Bertha and Vincent Ostrander, had two children, mom and a son, James Lester. As an adult James would go by the name Les in the family and by the name Jim at work. As kids they apparently got along well and shared many responsibilities on the farm. Before breakfast mom said she gathered the eggs from the hen house and her brother would milk the cows. Life was just subsisting from day to day.

During the best of times they didn't have much beyond the necessities so the Great Depression made things a whole lot worse. She told me that her and her brother would share a pair of skis when they went to school in the winter. They would each wear one ski when they went home. Mom said that her mom was a strict disciplinarian. To illustrate that point, she related a story of how she once stole an orange from a street vender because she was hungry and they didn't have any food at home. Grandma whipped her within an inch of her life and Mom never forgot that lesson. She told me that story one day after I came home from school and told her I had seen someone's answer to a test question while taking a test. She related how that was stealing and was just as wrong as her stealing that orange. Thank God she didn't whip me but she didn't need to. Her disapproval was punishment enough and I learned my lesson.

Mom's parents did not get along well and there was a lot of tension at home. Finally it reached a breaking point for mom. She quit school while in 8th grade and ran away from home. She was so lonely for love that she easily became a victim to any man who would speak nice to her and show her affection. At 15 she met a guy (Daddy told me his name but I don't remember it), married him (she lied about her age on the wedding license) and he abused her. She divorced him when she was 16. Unfortunately she didn't learn her lesson as she quickly hooked up with another guy who also abused her and she was divorced a second time by the time she was 17 years old.

So by the time she met Daddy she had lived a tough life. Daddy knew of her past and wanted her to know that he was different. He wasn't going to hurt her and was going to provide for her for the rest of her life which he did. As I was growing up I noticed that Daddy earned a lot of money and mom spent a lot of money. Daddy loved her and therefore he let her have most of what she wanted because she had such a hard life as a poor child. Fortunately he made good money which allowed him to treat her so royally.

Daddy was born Eugene Robert Estle Flynn on July 17, 1924 in Mitchell, South Dakota. He had 2 sisters, Zelda and Winnie, and a brother, Orvis. His brother Orvis was a year older than Daddy and had a heart ailment. Daddy said that his condition was really hard on the family. Everyone was hoping and praying that Orvis would pull through. Daddy's family was poor too, as were most families during the Great Depression. They got Orvis the best medical attention they could afford but it ended up not saving him. Orvis died of an enlarged heart in 1930 when he was only 9 years old. His death took a heavy toll on Daddy and his family. I remember growing up seeing Daddy cry whenever he remembered his brother and how much he suffered.

Jobs were hard to come by during the Great Depression so his parents, Elmo and Freda, moved the family to Michigan in the hopes that his dad would be able to find a job to support the family. He eventually got a job offer driving a truck but the family would have to move to Chicago. Grandma didn't want to leave Michigan because she liked it there. They had a big fight. Grandpa felt because of the economic hard times that he had to take the job offer as another one may not come along. So he left Grandma and went on to Chicago.

He got the job and like a dutiful husband, he sent the money home to Michigan. I know he hoped Grandma would forgive him for leaving her and the kids and would come to Chicago so they could be reunited. Grandma however couldn't forgive him for leaving the family. She kept the money but eventually divorced him. Daddy, as the only boy now in the family, became the bread winner. He got odd jobs while still in high school to support his mother and sisters. I never understood why Grandma didn't get a job during that time. Daddy never said but maybe she felt it was more important to be a stay-at-home-mom than to work.

While in high school at Pontiac High School in Pontiac, Michigan, Daddy excelled in engineering and math. He told me how his engineering teacher would have him teach the class when he (the teacher) had to go to a meeting or be away for a short time. Of course the other students gave Daddy a hard time about it, saying he was teacher's pet. Daddy took it all in stride as he wanted to be an engineer and looked at every opportunity to learn as a gift.

When he finished high school he joined the army (Company B, 842nd E. A. B.) and fought in World War II in the Pacific theater. He was a truck driver and an expert with a carbine rifle, attaining the rank of Tech 5. He frequently would go to the battlefield before the troops, setting up an interchangeable parts depot for the heavy trucks and equipment. He served in operations in the Eastern Mandates and Ryukyus and received the Victory Medal, Asiatic-Pacific Theater Ribbon with 2 bronze battle stars for the Battle of Guadalcanal and the Battle of Okinawa, 3 overseas service bars, and the Good Conduct Medal. He was honorably discharged in January 1946.

Daddy never talked much about the war. He didn't like it and said he was a fool hardy kid that really had no business being there. He went to do his patriotic duty to defend his country but said he was lucky he was not killed as he said he did a lot of foolish things (he never told me the details). He always said he was a cocky 18 year old kid who thought he couldn't die. He believed till the day he died that the main reason he survived was because God had plans for him (including my birth) that required it. I once asked him if he ever had to kill someone and he looked at me with a horrified expression, didn't answer, and walked away. I know if Daddy did kill someone during the war, he only did it in self defense. But I could tell that the whole war episode in his life was very painful.

After the war Daddy got a job driving car carriers for a while. With all his battle experience he drove a lot of trucks and heavy equipment. He did that for a while but he didn't really want that to be his permanent job. He wanted an engineering job. He eventually got on at a small manufacturing company in Pontiac, Michigan, as a mechanical engineer. He did the base mechanical drawings for a new product that would replace faucet assemblies on sinks. The product, called the "Dishmaster", would allow the user to wash dishes without putting their hands in soapy water. It was while he worked at this job that he met Mom.

They were introduced by mom's mother, Bertha. They dated for a few months and it was love at first sight. Daddy had a lot of hobbies, one of which was his Piper Cub plane. His fascination for flying must have been great as he somehow found the money to get his flying license and to buy a small plane. He loved to fly. He told me a number of times that he felt being alone in a plane is the most serene feeling a human being can have. You are so far away from any worries on the ground that it allows you to get everything back into its proper perspective. In fact, his and mom's first date was a date in the heavens, so to speak.

As I said before, he loved it but Mom told me she hated it. Mom was a consummate worrier. She not only worried about her own safety she also worried every time Daddy got into the plane. Throughout Mom's life she would get herself in a frizzy about just about anything. She told me that she told Daddy he would have to choose between her and the plane as he couldn't have both. Fortunately for me Daddy chose her, sold the plane, and never flew again.

He had a Harley Davidson motorcycle and actually loved it even more than his plane. He would sometimes go off with his best friend, who also had a Harley Davidson, and they would cycle across country to California. They would be gone for weeks on end leaving Mom to worry herself to death that something terrible had happened to him. Daddy told me later that after one of his trips she told him the same thing she had said about the plane except this time it was about the motorcycle. She said, 'Gene, it's either me or motorcycle. You can't have both.' So Daddy also got rid of his beloved Harley. He clearly loved Mom or he wouldn't have gotten rid of the two material things he loved the most in this world. He loved her completely and was willing to prove it. His selling of his motorcycle and plane certainly was a good start.

The Flynn family, however, didn't like Mom. They didn't buy the idea that she was abused in her previous relationships and maligned both her and Daddy during their courtship. They called her terrible names including whore. Daddy had to choose between Mom and his family. Lucky again for me he chose Mom. They got married January 17, 1948 in Bowling Green, Ohio, by a justice of the peace. They lived in Pontiac, Michigan at the time. None of Daddy's family was at the ceremony. Other than mom's parents, the only other people who were there was a couple who were their best friends. He was their best man and she was the maid of honor. Daddy was 23 and Mom was 21. They did truly love each other as their marriage lasted 36 years and ended only with Mom's death of cancer in March 1984.

Daddy was a hard working man, very smart, and had a great business sense. His hard work on the "Dishmaster" paid off for him as he became CEO of Manville Manufacturing when the founder, Charles Manville, died. Starting out he didn't make a lot of money. But he made enough for him and Mom to afford a small apartment on Huron Street in Pontiac across from the hospital where I was born.

They tried fervently to have children. Mom and Daddy had Rh factor blood problems. She was Rh- and Daddy was Rh+. They tried 7 times. Mom got pregnant but each time the fetus would abort as the blood would agglutinate in the fetus. This was before amniocentesis was known. Then a miracle happened on the eighth attempt. For some unknown reason, the placenta fixed itself and the blood didn't agglutinate. Mom carried me full term and I was born May 26, 1949 in Pontiac, Michigan. I was named Duane James Flynn: Duane after my Daddy's first boss, Duane Miller, and James after my mother's brother, James Lester.

My birth wasn't easy. Mom's water broke and she was in labor for two days before I was born. She was tired with all the hard labor and she told me the doctor had to use forceps to get me out, giving me two black eyes. They said I came out with clenched fists. I wasn't happy from the beginning. Both of us (Mom and me) were scrappers and that would show itself throughout both of our lives. So from the beginning, I knew I was special. I lived when the other fetuses didn't. In fact, Mom and Daddy tried 4 more times to give me a brother or sister to play with but Mom lost all four, aborting with fetal agglutination. In fact, the last pregnancy was a tubular pregnancy and when the doctor went into to remove the aborted fetuses, they both broke in his hand full of gangrene. Therefore I remained an only child. The whole idea that I survived guided me throughout my journey. I should have died with the others. Medically my birth was unexplainable. Trying to understand my survival would drive me throughout my journey. I would come to understand the full meaning of my survival.

After I was born we lived in that small apartment across the street from the hospital for a while. Mom took a picture of me in the crib and I was definitely a cute kid. I remember having "thin" hair but a cute swirl on top of my head. When I saw the pictures, I thought 'that's cute. It almost looks girly'.

Daddy was good at building things. He bought a piece of land on Orlando Street in Pontiac and decided to build a house. He and Mom built it with their own hands. It was a neat house. It was square, simple and roomy. It actually was about the size of a modern day garage. I loved it there. I made a lot of friends both in school and in the neighborhood. I attended K-1st grade at Wisner School near home.

Wisner Elementary School was a two story building with classrooms on the first floor and administration on the second floor. It had classes for grades K through 6th grade. One of the neatest things about Wisner School was that it had a football field next to it. Wisner Stadium was one of the largest stadiums in town and was used by many other schools in the community for their football games and special fund raising games. As a kid growing up, older kids (i.e. big kids) were always admired and it was the big kids who got to play football at Wisner Stadium. It was the dream of all kids to one day play football there. I dreamed of playing football there one day just like any other boy my age.

Mom would walk me to and from school each day as it was about ¼ mile from home. Half way to the school was a small grocery store where we would frequently stop and Mom would buy me some goodies. At one visit she bought me a gum ball. When I bit down on it, it shot down my throat, blocking my wind pipe. I started choking as I couldn't breathe. Mom started to panic. A stranger came into the store, quickly assessed the situation, picked me up by my feet, hung me upside down, stuck his finger down my throat, and pulled the gum ball free. I cried and was shaken up but fine. Mom was of course overjoyed that the stranger saved my life. She got his address and phone number, staying in contact with him over the years and sending him Christmas cards, until he died. As I look back at the situation, it clearly shows me God's hand protecting me. I know God had plans for me because He sent the kind stranger to the store at the very moment I was choking to save my life.

I started Kindergarten when I was 5 years old. I had a dog, Bing, who I dearly loved and who dearly loved me. He was a Shetland Sheep Dog. He wouldn't sleep anywhere but on my bed. I started missing a lot of days in school for being sick. Mom took me to the doctor and they determined that I was allergic to Bing's long hair. We ended up having to give Bing away and I thought I would die. It was a very traumatic experience. I cried for days. I eventually missed 109 days of Kindergarten, mostly due to my allergic reaction to Bing's long hair. I remember the last day of school my teacher got all my classmates together and asked them to vote as to whether I should pass to the 1st grade. They all said 'yes' and I passed. I know that I went on to the 1st grade because it was the teacher who passed me but it was neat that the class voted me to pass.

While attending Wisner School I got my first crush. Like most young boys I got a crush on one of my teachers. Her name was Miss Reynolds and she was my 1st grade teacher. I even would deliberately misbehave so she would make me sit next to her at the front of the class. She was smart though and caught on, eventually making me sit in the back, as far away from her as possible, when I misbehaved. I didn't like that at all and I quickly started to behave better. Misbehaving wasn't fun anymore.

Daddy's job was now head engineer. It allowed him to buy a nice house on Snow Apple Drive in a new subdivision in Clarkston, Michigan. I remember the house seemed HUGE to me. It had two bedrooms, 2.5 baths, living room, dining room, kitchen, utility room, a den, and the biggest yard in the neighborhood (the yard actually was two lots). It was at least 4 times bigger than the house on Orlando Street. I went to school at Clarkston Elementary. I loved school. I have always loved to learn and I made friends easily. It was while living there that I apparently started showing the first signs of something being wrong concerning my gender.

I remember Daddy and Mom taking me to the doctor when I was 7 years old. This trip to the doctor was different than the others. I remember I wasn't sick. The doctor took me to the back examining room and gave me a shot in my butt. I hated shots and I cried a good bit. Daddy came and picked me up to console me. When he picked me up, I was facing away from Daddy's face, leaning my head on Daddy's shoulder. Then I vividly remember the doctor facing Daddy and telling him, "He'll be normal now." Back then I obviously didn't know what being "normal" meant since I was only 7 years old. But the memory of the doctor's words has stayed with me my whole life. As I progressed in my journey years later, its true meaning became clearer to me. I must have been showing some characteristics of a girl (speech, mannerisms, requests, etc.) and what the doctor did was give me a hormone shot. The hormone shot, it seems, was to hopefully make me a normal boy. I don't remember doing or saying anything when I was 7 years old that was girly but I must have. This was the first sign that the "die was being cast".

Mom was very loving and we spent a lot of time together when I was a child. Mom clearly loved me and enjoyed having me with her. We did a number of things that traditionally would be things that girls would do with their moms. Looking back I think these things nurtured the feeling within me that I really was a girl and not a boy.

One was shopping. Mom loved to shop for clothes, especially dresses. So as a child, 5-10 years old, Mom would take me with her to the dress shop. I would sit still in a chair for hours as Mom would try on dresses. She would come out modeling them and ask me, her young son, if I thought Daddy would like it. She obviously was seeking a male opinion but a child of 5-10 years old usually doesn't have much fashion sense. I didn't, but loved going. I loved the feel of the dress material and being with women. The women store clerks couldn't believe how good I was. I never squirmed or fussed because I was taking it all in. To this day I can remember the layout of Mom's favorite dress shop, Winkleman's, in Pontiac: The dresses were in the front of the store on both sides. The center aisle was open with the 4 fitting rooms on each side, divided in half with a mirror. There were also benches for waiting dad's (and children) to sit near the fitting rooms. In the back of the dress shop was the cash register and clerk's offices. I can see it today as if I was there yesterday.

Another thing I did was helping in the kitchen. She let me help her cook and dry the dishes. At an early age (5 years old) I learned to help in the kitchen by drying pans. That later expanded to doing dishes (automatic dishwashers hadn't been invented yet), sweeping and mopping the floor, and helping cook. However the cooking part I still haven't mastered.

I remember fondly the hours that we spent coloring together and building houses with cards. For those unfamiliar with building houses with cards, let me briefly explain how it's done. You form a box by standing cards up on their edges in a square, leaning each card against the other. Then you add a card flat across each corner to give it support and strength. A second floor can be attempted which adds a challenge to the house building. We would build houses that would fill the whole floor of the living room. It was great fun.

Daddy played with me a lot when he was home, especially on weekends. I was very secure in his love for me. We played catch whenever the weather permitted and Daddy helped me build many projects for Cub Scouts and school projects. But my time with Mom was special time. I don't believe Mom ever wanted me to be a girl as I cannot remember her ever saying or doing anything that told me that. But now as I look back, I clearly identified with Mom during these years. Doing those things with Mom made her very happy and being with her made me very happy. I wonder now, though, if the frequent contact with female environments (i.e. dress shops) and doing female chores helped me form an alternate identity for myself.

From an early age I became a student of the Bible. At night for my bedtime story Daddy would read to me from a series of books by Uncle Arthur which took the Bible and put it into simple terms even a kid could understand. I loved it. I remember telling Daddy one night that I wanted to hear another story. He said, "It's midnight and time for bed". I was amazed that I wasn't even sleepy (but I'm sure he was) because I loved the stories so much. Throughout my adult life I carried this deep interest in the Bible with me, reading everything I could get my hands on which eventually led to my going to Duke Seminary. This deep interest in the Bible would serve me well later in my life. It would help bring me back to God when the church implied my life was unacceptable to God because I was living in sin by cross dressing.

Chapter 2
School Dreams

School was hard for me. Don't get me wrong. I was smart and I loved the intellectual challenges of learning and that love of learning has never left me. It has been a constant companion all through college and my graduate programs. I have done well academically. I graduated with honors from Waterford-Kettering High School, Drayton Plains, Michigan (1967); graduated 'cum laude' from Olivet College, Olivet, Michigan with a B.A. in Science (1971); graduated with an M.S., majoring in Entomology from the University of Georgia, Athens, Georgia including memberships in Alpha Chi and Sigma Zeta, Science Honoraries (1973). Getting good grades was not hard for me. It was fun. What was hard for me was hiding my true self.

The yard in Clarkston was huge. It was actually two lots so I was the envy of all the kids in the neighborhood because it was large enough to play football and baseball. So I had lots of friends. Daddy also built me a huge sandbox and bought me lots of trucks to play with. Kids came from all over (even neighborhoods outside the subdivision) to play in it. Moms would drop them off and we didn't know who they were. It was okay with me because I didn't care. I played with them anyway.

I never really liked playing with the trucks (I secretly wanted to play with dolls) but I enjoyed the friends that came over. So I played with them and filled the roll I was expected to fill, that of a nice friendly boy in the neighborhood. However I played with girls whenever I could.

Since my discovery with Grandma's earrings, my identification with girls increased along with becoming more and more uncomfortable with being a boy.

In gym class in school I felt out of place in the boy's locker room. I didn't like to expose myself to others and I detested my penis. I felt like a girl and that I didn't belong there. I became very protective of my private parts, not wanting anyone to see them. The boys in the locker room could care less as they were running around naked and flaunting their penises. It bothered me that I couldn't tell anyone how I felt. I just had to hide my feelings inside. After all boys are supposed to be boys and I was expected to act accordingly. I acted the part but I hated every minute of it.

During my school years through high school (1955-1967), there were always boys that were identified as queers and labeled such because they either didn't look boyish or they didn't do what was expected of boys which included being athletic and participating in sports.

I never knew if I was athletic because Mom would never let me go out for the teams. She always told me she was afraid that I would get hurt and reminded me that I was the only baby that survived and that she could never have another. So I didn't conform by doing what was expected of boys (i.e. go out for sports) so I was labeled as queer and was picked on by some of my classmates. Because of these ribbings, I resented Mom stopping me from going out for sports. I told her that it made life in school hard but she wouldn't budge in her decision. I really didn't want to participate in the sports but I did want my schoolmates to quit picking on me. It was probably better that I didn't try out as I most likely would have been picked on even more when I failed to make the team. Oh well, I guess it was a no win situation no matter which way I decided.

Since athletics were not part of my school activities, I focused on my studies. I became well known all throughout both primary and secondary school as a nerd. I studied well and got good grades. Studying was fun and it also allowed me an avenue to bury my pains. I was friendly to all kids even the hoods of my day. The hoods were those kids who smoked and wore black leather jackets. They were looked down on by the other kids and very frequently were at the principal's office for breaking some rule. I didn't have a black leather jacket or smoke but they liked me anyway. I think it was because I treated them with respect.

Most of them didn't do well in school so they were tagged by other students as being dumb and were picked on. I identified with them for being picked on and not understood. I believed they could pass so I offered to help those that were in my classes with their studies. They were shocked that anyone cared about them and were eager for me to tutor them. After I did my own homework, I worked with them during study hall to improve their grades. And, with my help, the grades of many of them not only improved but they were able to get the best grades they ever got.

They were very happy and, of course, the teachers were happy. I know the teachers wanted to help them but they just didn't have the time. As an added bonus, they became my protectors.

Yes, if anyone picked on me, they were right there and offered to pummel them for me. I always declined but it was nice to know they liked me and were there to protect me. I was always afraid someone would discover my secret that I wanted to be a girl. It was neat too that they never tried to change me into one of them. They always accepted me for who I was, never questioning my appearance or motives. Of course I did the same with them.

I have always had a caring, compassionate character (a female characteristic but I didn't know it then). This led to one of the most successful things I did in high school—I secretly tried out for the track team and I didn't tell Mom.

I wasn't fast nor did I have long endurance but I thought I could run ¼ mile. It didn't require you to be real fast like the 100 yard dash or to have long endurance like the mile. It ended up that during tryouts I ran an okay ¼ mile but I wasn't among the fastest. Coach liked me so he asked me if I would be the track manager. The track manager was the person in charge of providing the rubdowns, equipment care, give support at track meets, keep records of each team member's performances, and report the meet results to the paper.

I thought about it and was honored that he asked me to do such an important job. Even though I wouldn't be able to run, I could contribute to the team, get those idiots at school off my back, and participate in a way that would not risk injury. I decided to do it and told Mom. She said okay and, as I suspected, was most happy with the fact that to her it didn't seem to be dangerous.

Being a manager was easy for me and I did well. I was track manager for two years and received honors and accolades from the players, coach, and the parents of the players for the care I gave their sons. I loved doing it but at the time I didn't fully connect that its nurturing nature was why I loved doing it and did well. Looking back I realized I actually treated my track classmates like that of a mother, nurturing them, ensuring that they got the best care.

When I went to basketball and football games in high school, like other boys, I liked to watch the cheerleaders. But my looking took on a different nature than theirs. They were looking at them because they were the cutest girls in school and they all wanted to date them. I didn't have any desire to date them. I wanted to look like them. I secretly wanted to be pretty like them, wear their dresses and be admired like they were. The cheerleaders were always the prettiest most popular girls in school (all our cheerleaders were girls). They also were some of the meanest girls in school but I thought if I could be one I could be the first kind one. Yet, all those desires had to remain a secret in my heart. I could never let anyone know. I wanted so desperately to be liked and revealing my secret to anyone would make me hated and despised even more than I already was.

At home I found myself cross dressing whenever I could when I was alone. Whenever Mom went next door to visit our neighbor Ilene or go to the store, I would go into her closet, put her clothes on and sit by the window. I was content to just sit there and feel the dress or skirt on my body and dream I was a girl. It all felt right and it gave me peace in my soul when I was cross dressed. Interestingly, I learned exactly how much time was needed to undress, put her clothes back on the hangers, and get my clothes back on before she came in the door. I never got caught. I was always successful in putting her clothes exactly where they were in the closet and getting my boy clothes back on before she got home. Also, since I was at peace the whole time I was dressed, I never sweat on her dresses or tops so they never smelled which aided me in my secret activity.

Whenever I dressed up, I would experiment with different clothes combinations and soon became very adept at what clothes went together. Luckily Mom's clothes fit me perfectly as we were the same size during the time I was in high school which made the illusion even better. I would even put on one of her bras, stuff the cups with a pair of her nylons, and dream I had breasts. I would even caress them in a seductive way, pretending I was dancing in front of men.

Some of Mom's most beautiful clothes were her furs. During the 50's and 60's when I was growing up, women commonly wore furs and Mom was no exception. She had a beautiful ¾ length fur coat that she and Daddy called a Lion's Paw Mink. The fur pattern was like a lions paw and was unbelievably beautiful. She also had a mink wrap with the head made into a clip that held the wrap on your shoulder. Mom wore both the lions paw mink coat and mink wrap frequently in the winter. When I saw her wear them I had to watch myself that I didn't drool too much. When I cross dressed in the winter I would not miss an opportunity to put each one of them on and swoon in front of the mirror. In my eyes, these furs were the ultimate female clothes.

Mom's earrings were either clip-on or screw. Few women had pierced ears then. Mom was fearful of getting her ears pierced because she falsely believed it would be painful. She didn't get pierced ears until many years after I left the house to live on my own. She did it with Dad's sister Zelda. Since I had a penchant for earrings (ever since my discovery at Grandma's house), I practiced putting them on whenever I could. The clip-ons were easy but they hurt your ears after a while since you couldn't adjust the pressure of the clip. I liked the screw back earrings the best. They were the prettiest anyway, usually rhinestones, pearls, or diamonds. The screw backs were adjustable so you had to practice adjusting the screw to just the right tightness to keep the earring on and yet to not hurt your ear. Soon I got pretty adept at where to set the screw. If the time that Mom was going to be gone wouldn't allow me to change clothes, I would just put earrings on, frequently visiting the mirror in the bathroom to admire how they looked. Whenever I put a pair of the screw back earrings on, I would notice how tight the screw was BEFORE I moved it so I could adjust the screw back to the same spot when I put it back. Again, Mom never knew anything was amiss.

Mom liked to talk on the phone a lot, especially with good friends. Frequently she would talk for hours. One time when she had been on the phone for a while I decided to try on one of her dresses that I had been admiring. I went into her bedroom, got the dress and went back into my bedroom and closed the door. I took off my clothes, unzipped it, stepped into it, pulled it up in front and then pulled the back up so I could zip it up. When the zipper went to the top I got a rush. It felt so good. As I usually do when putting Mom's clothes on, I left it on as long as I could.

I kept the door slightly open so I could hear Mom on the phone and listen for when it sounded like she was getting ready to hang-up. Then I would quickly get the dress off and return it to her closet. Sure enough, about a half hour after putting the dress on, I heard her sound like she was getting ready to hang-up. I reached up the back of the dress to unzip it but to my horror I couldn't get the zipper down. I reached over my head to pull the back of the dress up so I could get a better grasp of the zipper but it wouldn't budge. I had apparently sweated and the zipper was stuck. Now I was stuck too. I couldn't get it off! I started to panic. What was I going to do? When Mom got off the phone, she called my name and wanted to know where I was. I sheepishly said I was in the bedroom (my bedroom door was ajar so she could hear me fine). She asked me to come out and I told her I couldn't. I started to cry and she heard me. She quickly came and opened my door the rest of the way. I hid behind the door, stupidly thinking she wouldn't see me. I was so afraid of what she would do when she saw me in her dress. When she saw me she was indeed angry but not overly angry. She asked me, "Why are you in my dress?" I said I was just experimenting and the zipper got caught. She told me to turn around and she proceeded to unzipped it so I could take it off. I asked her not to tell Daddy as I was afraid of a spanking. She agreed she wouldn't tell him if I promised not to do it again. I said I would try (I couldn't lie. I told myself that I would try not to get caught again but I knew I would continue to put more of her dresses on. They just felt too good). When I dressed up, I never thought it would be possible to ever become a woman. I just accepted that I could never be a woman as I was born a boy but I dreamed of being forced to be a girl.

For some reason I found great excitement and solace in those dreams. One of my favorite dreams was where I was taken forcibly by a gang of boys into a building. In the building was a huge machine. At the top of it was a large hole. They took me up onto a ledge above the machine and pushed me so that I fell into the hole and couldn't escape. I then became the victim of the machine. The machine did not kill me. That was not what the machine did. Instead, it spit me out the other end and I came out a girl.

I dreamed that dream many times each week for about 10 years. I would almost always have a wet dream along with it. The idea of being forced to be a girl gave me a sexual high. I really hated being a male and being forced to be a woman in the dreams took the responsibility off my shoulders. It was out of my control so I suppose it made me feel better about it.

Daddy and Mom attended church regularly. I remember as a child we would attend a Baptist church in town. They would always tell me that God loved me and encouraged me to attend Sunday school. Because Mom and Daddy smoked and occasionally drank with friends they were asked to leave the Baptist Church. In fact, the leaders of the church came out to our house one day and told Mom and Daddy that they had a member of the church follow them for weeks. They told them that they would have to stop drinking, smoking, and get rid of all their friends if they wanted to be a member of their church and go to heaven. Mom and Daddy never went back.

They wanted to go to church and tried numerous different churches but didn't like them. Then they visited Christ Lutheran Church in Waterford, Michigan. They really liked the pastor, Pastor Anderson, and joined. Since we were not baptized, we all got baptized (sprinkled) on Palm Sunday, 1957. I don't remember much about it except Daddy and I had to wear a suit and Mom got to wear a pretty dress. I envied her because I wanted to wear a pretty dress too.

I spent a lot of time with my Maternal Grandma (her name was Bertha Reynolds) as well as my Paternal Grandmother. She loved to fish and she taught me how to bait a hook with a worm (yuck) and 'still fish' from a boat with a bobber on a line. She lived off of Orchard Lake in Pontiac, Michigan and her and Grandpa owned a small motor boat. We would go out into the lake and 'still fish' for hours, catching bluegill and perch. We would then bring them home, clean them, and have them for dinner. I loved the taste of fresh fish but I didn't like to remove the main back bone and ribs. I wasn't good at it and frequently would swallow a small bone, scratching my throat and then it would hurt for days until it healed. To this day whenever I order fish at a restaurant I always order filets. We would always look for any excuse to fish and one day Grandpa agreed to take us up to Bay City and get us tickets to fish out on Lake Huron. We were so excited we couldn't stand it!

Grandpa drove us up to outside Bay City and we got our tickets to the fishing boat. We got our gear together along with a giant cooler we hoped to fill with fish. We went out on Lake Huron and I remember it was a lot colder than I thought it would be. It was cold but that was okay as my mind was on catching fish! Grandma and I sat beside each other on one of the sides of the boat. Grandma changed my leader into a double leader so I would have two hooks. We had bought a large jar of night crawlers for bait so we were ready. She baited my hooks and I let them down into the water. The boat moved up and down so much you really couldn't use a bobber. You had wait for the tug on the line to tell you that you had a bite.

I no sooner got my line in the boat and I got so hard a tug on my line that it almost pulled it out of my hand. Grandma helped me pull it up and sure enough I had not only one fish but one on each hook – two fish! That was why it pulled so hard. I was thrilled to death. We took them off the hooks, put them in the cooler, baited my hooks again, and fished again. We fished on the boat for about 4 hours and filled our cooler with fish. It was such great fun. I was surprised that I had so much fun even though I wasn't dressed up.

Another fishing episode was even more exciting. Grandma, Grandpa and me went to a small lake in the interior of the Lower Peninsula of Michigan to fish. I don't remember the name of the lake or the town only that it was a pretty good sized inland lake. It was probably a good mile across the long axis. We went to bed early as Grandma wanted to get up at 4am and be on the lake as soon as there was light. I had never gotten up at 4am before but I didn't think anything about it because I was excited about the day of fishing. We got our gear into the boat and set off at about 4:30am at the break of daylight. I was given the task of rowing the boat and Grandma was the navigator. She directed us across the lake to some coves to start. We stopped at numerous coves and 'still fished' for hours but caught very few fish.

Grandma kept moving us hoping to find a good spot. Soon I was getting blisters on my hands but I kept rowing. Finally about two hours before dark we found the spot. When we put our lines into the water we immediately began to catch fish. We were having so much fun that we lost track of time. I noticed that it was getting dark and told Grandma we needed to head for shore. She didn't want to stop. She said we would fish for a few more minutes. A few minutes later it was totally dark. We couldn't even see the shoreline. When we tried to get our bearings as to which direction to go, we realized we were lost. I envisioned us being stranded all night on the lake. With it dark we couldn't see any landmarks. Grandma told me to row in a certain direction toward what she thought was the shore but we never got to shore. I could tell Grandma was now getting worried. I said a silent prayer to God. I told him, "Lord. We're lost. Please help us find the shore." No sooner did I finish the prayer and Grandma noticed a light moving on the shoreline. She told me to row toward it so we could ask them for directions home. I eagerly rowed to the light even though my hands were now raw with blisters. When we got to the shore we were shocked. The person waving the lantern was Grandpa. He noticed we were not back so he got a lantern and gave us a beacon to lead us home. When we got to shore both of us got out of the boat, hugged Grandpa, and cried for joy. I firmly believe to this day that God sent Grandpa to be our beacon because His hand was on both of us, bringing us to safety.

After Grandpa retired, Grandma and Grandpa sold their trailer near the lake and their boat. They then bought a cottage near Bay City, Michigan. I never went fishing with Grandma again and I missed it. Those were special times that I will always remember. Mom and Daddy would take me up to the cottage and I would stay for a weekend. While there I would, of course, eventually find a way to satisfy my desire to dress as a girl.

Grandma's clothes were too small for me (she was only 4 foot tall) and I was never left alone long enough to wear them anyway. But she did have a tube of raspberry lipstick in the bathroom. During one visit when I went to the bathroom I decided to try some on. I did and loved how it looked. Before I left the bathroom I wiped it off with Kleenex and put the soiled Kleenex in the toilet. But in my haste, I forgot to flush it. Grandma found the Kleenex in the toilet later that day while one of her friends was visiting. She asked her friend if she had used her lipstick. Her friend said she didn't remember but must have and apologized. Grandma wasn't happy that someone had used her lipstick. But she forgot about it in a couple of days. I felt bad that I made Grandma get angry at one of her friends, who was innocent of doing anything wrong.

On Christmas day 1960, I got a shocking surprise. I was celebrating Christmas at Grandma Flynn's house in Pontiac, Michigan (yes, the same house where I had the infamous earring discovery). After dinner, we all gathered in Grandma's small living room to sing Christmas carols. Before we started singing, I asked for everyone's attention as I had an announcement. I don't recall what it was, but I do remember Uncle Dick's response to me stating that I had an announcement. He loudly said, "Duane is having a sex change". I was in shock.

Uncle Dick was a horrific kidder but I felt myself turning red as I thought, "Oh My God. Someone knows my secret." I tried not to look scared (even though I was petrified) and I said, "No, I am not having a sex change." Uncle Dick quickly retorted, "You sure could have fooled me." In my mind I kept telling myself, "How did he know I wanted to be a girl?" I am mystified, even today, at his statement. Uncle Dick was very observant and no dummy. I firmly believe that somehow he knew. The whole incident was one of those prophetic moments that you can't explain. I only know that it had a big impact on me. Everyone laughed at the situation except me. I didn't know how to laugh because it was true. I did want sex change surgery. I wondered if my inability to laugh gave me away even more to the family. No one asked me any questions later so I guess they took it as one of Uncle Dick's jokes. I didn't though. I remembered it with some fear.

While watching TV in the early 1960's I saw something that quickly grabbed my attention. It was a news program that was talking about Christine Jorgensen, a man who had sex change surgery in Denmark—a man who was now a beautiful woman. I found myself staring at the TV. She was gorgeous. I can still remember the excitement I felt when I saw her picture. I wondered – could that be me? Could I have surgery, become a woman and look gorgeous like her? Up until then I didn't know that there were other men who wanted to be girls. Now I dreamed about someday getting enough money to have the same surgery. But I still needed to keep my dreams from my family and to myself.

In 1961, I became eligible to start Confirmation Classes at my local church. In the Lutheran denomination 12 year old boys and girls take a series of classes (10 weeks) taught by the pastor, teaching them about what it means to be a Christian, the meaning of communion, and the history of the Lutheran denomination. Among other things we had to learn Martin Luther's explanations of the 10 commandments. It was an intense 10 weeks but I loved every minute of it. As I mentioned before, I thrived on church and Bible history and I ended up tied with a girl in the class for the highest grade.

After completing the 10 week course, our class of confirmants stood before the local church where they confirm their faith from the promise their parents made when they were baptized as an infant. It was a very moving experience for me and opened the door for me to have a life changing dream.

I had not had communion yet and was told to wait to take it until our local church was scheduled to have it the next time. This is because the Lutheran Church believes that one should not take communion until they understand the meaning of it. Otherwise the spiritual meaning of the sacramental "meal" is lost. Therefore children raised in the denomination don't take it until after they have completed confirmation. I finished confirmation on Palm Sunday so the next opportunity for me take communion was our scheduled communion on Maundy Thursday.

Unknown to me, the three of us (Mom, Daddy, and me) were invited by my Uncle Les and Aunt Lois (my Mom's brother and his wife) to go to a special Palm Sunday Service at their church. We went and they offered an open communion (that means it is open to anyone- those who are members of that church and those who are not members).

The service was very moving and I asked Mom and Daddy if I could take communion. They talked it over and said why not. I had finished confirmation therefore I knew what it meant. I went up and had my first communion and again, I was touched and moved. That night I had my life changing dream.

In the dream I was kneeling next to my bed praying to God to spare my life. I had a painting of Jesus, done when He first started His ministry, hanging over the head of my bed. It was one of those paintings that the eyes followed you everywhere you were in the room. The painting was very vivid in the dream except it was behind me as I knelt at the edge of the bed instead of on my right. I apparently had been told that I had an incurable disease and I was going to die. That is traumatic for a 12 year old kid. I was scared and I was asking God to spare my life. I said, "Lord, I'm too young to die. Please don't let me die."

After I made my request, a clear voice came from behind me, from the picture of Jesus, saying, "How can you preach my Word if you're dead." After I heard the voice of Jesus reassure me that I was not going to die, I heard another voice, outside the dream, yell my name – DUANE! I immediately woke up and went into Mom and Daddy's room and said, "What do you want?" Daddy said, "I didn't call for you". I told him I clearly heard him call my name. He repeated that he did not call my name. He then asked me if I had a dream. I told about my dream and he said he thought that the voice I heard was God's waking me up. He said we would talk about it in the morning.

In the morning we talked about the dream and he suggested I tell the pastor. We called and made an appointment and went to see him a couple days later. I told him the dream. He looked amazed and asked me if I remembered from confirmation the story of the prophet Samuel's call. I told him yes. He said he thought that many parts of my dream were very much like that of Samuel's call. He said that it could very well be God calling me into the ministry. He told me to continue to pray, be alert, and if it is a calling to ministry then God will confirm it by other signs.

Wow! God could be calling me into the ministry. That was exciting. Then I realized that it didn't make sense. I was struggling with my gender identity. How could God want a mixed up boy/girl in His ministry to the world. Maybe God made a mistake and someone else was supposed to get the dream. Yet the thought intrigued me. If this was God's call to the ministry, I needed to get my act together. I decided that from that day on my future profession was going to be a pastor.

I didn't experiment with makeup much during my junior high and high school years. The fear of being caught was too strong to risk but I did get caught once at home trying on Mom's lipsticks, totally due to stupidity.

Mom and Daddy had gone somewhere. And while they were gone for some reason I decided to experiment with some of Mom's many lipsticks. Mom probably had between 15-20 lipsticks. She had them in every color imaginable. Lipstick to me was the ultimate makeup of a woman. I knew that lipstick would dry after being on for a while and that most were hard to remove once they dried. The whole idea of putting lipstick on and not being able to remove it excited me. I'm sure it is again tied into the idea that I would have to then dress and be a woman (which I wanted) and the decision was out of my hands. That thought made me both excited and scared.

I tried on most of Mom's lipsticks, looked at myself in the mirror for about 30 seconds for each and then quickly removed it with a Kleenex. I always put the lipstick soiled Kleenex in the toilet and flushed it away, eliminating the evidence. But this time Mom and Dad came home early and, in my rush to get the lipstick off, I forgot to flush it.

Mom immediately went to the bathroom to pee and found it. I heard her call to Daddy to come and to see it. I could see the main bathroom mirror from my bedroom and I can still see Daddy to this day, looking in the toilet with his hands behind his back. I knew I was in trouble. I waited in my bedroom. Sure enough Daddy knocked and wanted to come in.

He came in, sat next to me on the bed, and proceeded to ask me about the lipstick soiled Kleenex in the toilet. I told him I was just experimenting (that became my pat answer any time I got caught doing girly things). I thought that was a good line and it was true. I was experimenting. He accepted it but he told me to never do it again. He told me that boys should feel uncomfortable wearing girly things including dresses and makeup. I didn't feel uncomfortable which made me wonder even more if there was something wrong with me. I told him I would try not to do it again (Again, I knew I would do it again so I didn't lie when I said I would try, which I did half-heartedly). I was never so scared. I really thought the gig was up. But I got off and I got off without a spanking. I decided after that incident that I would definitely become much more careful. I also decided, then and there, that I would make sure that I never got caught again by Mom and Daddy and I never was.

All through school I admired the girls. Not so much as potential dates, but, like the cheerleaders, I admired their clothes, makeup, and I wanted to be one. When I was in 6th grade and the girls started wearing makeup to school, I was jealous for I wanted to wear makeup so badly. I used this time as a learning experience and made mental notes about their clothes combinations and how they did their makeup.

Now I know that during that time, I was, in my mind, trying to learn how to be a girl. I was, I guess, going through female puberty, through my learning observations. Today I am told I am a smart dresser and I believe that all started with my observations of the girls in 6th grade.

I grew up in Clarkston, Michigan, going to Clarkston Elementary School (2nd – 5th grade), and Clarkston Junior High School (6th and part of 7th grade).

While in 7th grade in Clarkston Junior High School I took my first drafting class. Daddy was a draftsman and excellent engineer so I asked him if he would help me do my drawings. He was thrilled to help me and I got straight A's in class. It was the most fun I had in school. I know the fun was a combination of getting A's but also of doing it with Daddy. We bonded more during those sessions doing the drafting drawings than at any other time in my life. They are memories I will hold dear for the rest of my life. It was then that I decided that after I finished high school I was going to go college and be an architect. Yep, I was changing my future profession. I was now going to be an architect and design big churches. Surely God would understand if I didn't become a minister. With my gender dysphoria I felt it was better if I became an architect instead. I could still serve Him that way and surely He would be happy with me.

I knew a lot of kids in school and my church, Calvary Lutheran Church, was also in Clarkston. When I was in 6th grade, Daddy and Mom bought a new house in Pontiac so we moved to a new school district with my new school being Pierce Junior High in Drayton Plains. I went there through the rest of 7th grade and 8th grade then I went down the street to the high school, Waterford-Kettering. I wanted to take college prep courses in 9th grade and Pierce Junior High didn't have them so I got to take them at the High School. Nothing memorable happened at Pierce Junior High. I didn't make many friends so it was fortunate that after I moved I was still friends with kids from Clarkston, especially those I saw each Sunday at church.

There was a girl at my church in Clarkston that was really pretty and sweet. Her name was Sue. Because she was so pretty I kept looking at her every time I could, admiring her natural beauty and wishing I looked like her. She liked me too so I risked it and asked her to the Junior High Prom. She said yes and I was thrilled. I had just gotten my driving permit and was excited about taking a girl out on a date. This was my first real date. When I picked her up at her house her mom invited me in for a few minutes as Sue wasn't ready yet. We talked for a few minutes and then Sue came out. She looked fabulous. Her hair was in an up do and she had on the cutest light blue straight dress that had a pretty flower imprint in it.

To my surprise her mom gave me a gift. I told her she didn't need to do that but she smiled and said she was happy to as it was Sue's first date too. I took off the paper and found a lipstick box. I didn't know what to expect. Surely they didn't really buy me lipstick? Part of me was excited but I didn't want to give myself away as I was dressed in this very dapper tuxedo. So I made a joke and said, "Oh Boy! Just what I wanted—a new tube of lipstick". Her mom laughed and broke the silence by saying, "You are so cute. No, it's not lipstick. That was the only box I had to put the gift in." I smiled and opened the box, finding a very nice pen and pencil set. Little did she know how much her little box thrilled me. The date went okay and I enjoyed time with Sue but most of the time I was looking at her dress, her beautiful face and hair, admiring them.

While I was in high school prom time came and to my surprise, a girl from Clarkston High School that I knew at church asked me if I would take her to her prom. I said yes because I really liked her. Then a girl from my high school that I really liked name Yvonne asked me if I would take her to our prom. I never imagined that both proms would be on the same night so I said yes to both girls. I realized the day before the prom that both proms were on the same night! What was I going to do? I couldn't go to both proms as I couldn't be in two places at the same time. I liked both girls and didn't want to tell them that I had screwed up and made two dates for the same night. I would never live that down. If I could only go to one, I would have preferred the one with Yvonne at my school. But I didn't have the guts to tell the other girl no.

I prayed to God for an answer and God answered my prayer, sort of. Yvonne called the day before the prom and said she was sick and would not be able to go. I was disappointed but at least my dilemma was solved. Now I only had one date and that was for the Clarkston High School Prom. I was so relieved. I went with the girl and she was very sweet. But again I couldn't help looking at the beautiful prom dresses and wishing I was wearing one instead of concentrating on my date. When I took her home she thanked me for the evening, smiled, and we never dated again. I don't remember if she ever talked to me again even though we went to the same church. I have no other recollection of her.

From the outside, it seemed Mom and Daddy seemed oblivious to what was going on with me. Since they were so conservative I didn't feel comfortable approaching the subject of my gender dysphoria with them. But then again they never confronted me with it either. After being busted with mom's lipstick and not pursuing traditional male interests, I would have thought they would have said something but they didn't. I mean, after all, their only son was clearly not happy and didn't have traditional male features and interests. Why Dad never approached me about it is a mystery. It may have been that they both thought I would grow out of it and things would work out in the end. I do know that neither of them was comfortable with confrontation. Whenever they talked to me in a disciplinary setting or spanked me, they were uncomfortable and dreaded it. So maybe by not saying anything, they were trying to avoid an uncomfortable subject.

My church (Calvary Lutheran Church) was very conservative, teaching that it was an abomination to God if a man dressed like a woman as stated in Deuteronomy 22:5 – "A woman must not wear men's clothing, nor a man wear women's clothing for the Lord your God detests anyone who does this" [NIV]. The King James Version (KJV) says it is an abomination. I was scared what God was going to do to me. But I couldn't stop. I was so confused. I prayed many nights, "Lord, take this desire to be a girl from me as I don't want to anger you". Then the next night I would pray, "Lord, turn me into a girl so I can be happy". I knew that my heart's desire was to be a girl but I was conflicted with being born a male and the expectations that came along with it. My thoughts always came back to the dream of wanting to be what I felt I was inside, a girl. I kept hoping that that somehow, someday, I could find a way to make my dream come true.

Chapter 3
Losing Myself in Alcohol

My gender identity confusion seemed to be never ending. I suffered so much inner pain all through school. Everywhere I went, in school or in public, whenever I saw an attractive girl or woman, my heart yearned. Not to go to bed with them but to look like them. I didn't know what lust was because I never had it. No matter where I was or what I was doing it was the same. Whether shopping, watching TV, going to a movie – it didn't matter. When I saw an attractive girl or woman all I wanted was to look like them.

My SAT scores and graduation position was high enough that I could go to just about any college I wanted to. Before, when I wanted to be a minister I had planned on going to Augustana Theological Seminary outside of Chicago, Illinois. But now that I wanted to be an architect I applied to three colleges that had good architectural schools. I don't remember what the other two colleges were, but I was accepted to Michigan State University in East Lansing, Michigan right away. Many of my high school friends were going there so I immediately accepted. It just felt right. I wouldn't be far from home and it had a great architectural school. Daddy taught me everything he knew so I was good in engineering. Because of that I planned on applying to the Engineering program after I completed my first two years. Again I convinced myself that surely God would be happy if I designed churches and maybe wouldn't strike me down for wanting to be a girl in private. It would be our little secret.

I entered Michigan State in the fall of 1967, lived in East Shaw Hall and shared a dorm room with another student. My first roommate was okay as far as roommates go but I really wanted to live alone because it was too risky to dress up in a dorm especially with a roommate. If anyone caught me it would be mortifying. So I restrained myself for six months while my application for a private room was being reviewed. It was one of the hardest six months I had to endure up to that time. I was going through terrible withdrawals. I couldn't concentrate on studying and my grades were declining. I was afraid I would flunk out before I finished my first year! Finally I was approved for a private room. I happily and quickly moved to my private room. The first night I remember dressing up and the feeling of elation and relief that overcame me was unbelievable. The elation was as if I had won a million dollars! There were always risks of getting caught even in a private room but at least I was alone in my room and the only other person who had a key was the Resident Manager but he usually knocked before he entered.

My grades immediately improved and I felt better. In my gender confusion, I was constantly trying to reconcile my religious upbringing with my feelings. I tried hard to act like a guy and to like girls. I could fake it well but I was afraid people could see through me. Yes, I liked girls okay but I would go out with them so I could learn from them not so I could find a possible life partner. I wanted to learn everything about them, especially their movements. Even if opportunities came up to go to bed with a girl, I couldn't do it for two reasons. Number one was because my religious upbringing would not allow me to have sex outside of marriage and, number two, I felt like a girl so I couldn't get 'johnny' up. Even after marrying two very fine women, I had trouble getting an erection. So the only way I could cope with this conflict was to regularly masturbate. If I didn't masturbate the pain down between my legs became unbearable. Therefore I masturbated every night, all my life from puberty through my marriage years.

When the opportunity allowed it, I would dress in some article of female clothing while masturbating. Half the time I would dream I was a woman enticing a man and the other half of the time I would visualize myself being forced to be a woman. I don't believe the feel of the article of clothing itself against my body was what allowed me to orgasm.

A fetish is sexual arousal initiated by not only touching an article, frequently clothing, but also seeing the actual article or a picture of it. I don't believe I had a fetish for women's clothes. For me it was more than touching or seeing the clothes. I believe, for me, the clothes only complimented the true reason for my arousal, which was the fantasy of being a woman and being attractive to a man. So my orgasm was associated with making love, not with an article of clothing.

By this time I had accepted that I was probably transsexual but hadn't fully embraced it. I was torn. Part of me thought I was just a habitual cross dresser and could stop and the other part of me believed I was a woman trapped in a man's body.

The part of me that believed I was a transsexual dreamed of being a woman but didn't know how I could ever afford the $15,000-$30,000 that was required at that time to have the surgery. That part of me hoped that I could save the money after I finished college and got a job. But that would take such a long time and I didn't know if I could hold out.

The part of me that thought I was a habitual cross dresser was hooked on the dreams in which I am forced to be a woman. Now my dreams usually went like this: I would meet a natal woman (that is, one who was born a woman) who, when she found out I wanted to be a woman, would bind me and force me into womanhood. She would force me to wear a bra that had a padlock on it for which she had the only key which would not allow me to remove it. She would then force me to put on a very restrictive corset which forced my body into a beautiful, voluptuous shape. My hair then would be permanently cut and curled into a very feminine hairdo. After being dressed and having a feminine coiffure, she would put makeup on me including lipstick that would dry instantly and could not be removed. All of this would then give me no choice but to live as a woman for the rest of my life.

In college I would go the Library and checkout and photocopy every article from every book I could find on transvestites and transsexuals. I devoured information about both. I desperately wanted to know all I could about them. I found and read Christine Jorgensen's autobiography three times. I just couldn't get enough of it. It meant so much to me to know that there was someone else out there who was born a man who had confusion about their gender identity.

Like most cross dressers, I went through various cycles of purging tied to guilt. As I struggled with my gender identity, the guilt I felt increased. "If I just get rid of the clothes I won't be tempted to cross dress", I reasoned. I threw away two separate wardrobes while in college, hoping to stop the urge to cross dress even though all my readings about my condition said that purging never helped. I told myself that I would be the first to do it. It didn't work. After a month or so I would go out and buy another wardrobe. My inner desires to be a woman were too intense to ignore. Each time I went out to buy clothes and makeup I became more and more afraid of being found out. I knew that drag show 'girls' did it all the time but they had a cover. I didn't have a cover.

As a freshman at Michigan State University there was a Miss Red Cedar Pageant. All the participants of this pageant were men living in the dorms or fraternities that bordered on the Red Cedar River, of which East Shaw Hall was one. The men would dress like women and compete in a pageant. The winner would be chosen by campus students who watched the participants 'strut their stuff' and perform their talent. I wanted so badly to enter but I was so scared. I didn't feel I was pretty as a woman and just couldn't stand it if people laughed at me. I knew the others were doing it as a spoof and most were content in their skin as men but if I entered, I would be entering because <u>I wanted to be a woman</u>. It would have been serious for me and I was too afraid.

I did go to the pageant and saw the participants. None of them were pretty as they were spoofing women. But if I had entered, I would have done my very best to portray the woman I felt myself to be which included shaving my legs and chest, especially if I wore a low cut top as most of them did. Because I would have had a bare chest and legs I know I would have stood out. The thought of everyone watching me and laughing was more than I could bear. Deep down my inner self wanted to do it—the opportunity to dress up with all the outfits. Wow! But the other part of me said no because of the fear of being laughed at. Looking back, I'm glad I didn't do it but then again, I wonder if it would have helped me be more understanding of who I really was. That is what happened to me in the pageant in 2008 which I will discuss later in Chapter 6.

As is true for most transgendered people, there is a constant struggle internally, trying to conform our actions to our biological sex. Shortly after the Miss Red Cedar Pageant I decided to rush a fraternity. I told myself that if I could join a fraternity they would make a man out of me. The fraternity I chose was Phi Sigma Kappa and I was accepted to go through the evaluation process.

The fraternity I was rushing was a well known fraternity on campus. It was one of the few fraternities on campus that was known for having members that had good GPA's. During one of the rushing activities we had to go to a sorority and take a note to them.

There were seven pledges including me so we all went to the sorority. We knocked on the door. When one of the sorority sisters answered the door, she asked us why we were there. We told her what fraternity we were rushing and that we were told by the president of the fraternity to come to their sorority and present the note. She smiled and said she already knew as our fraternity president had already called them. She told us to go inside. Once inside, the pledge who had the note from the president, gave it to one of the sorority sisters. She read it and smiled. She got some of the other sisters together and they talked about it. Come to find out, the note requested one of the sisters to kiss one of the pledges (Paul) on the cheek, leaving a 'kiss mark' from her lipstick. Paul happened to be the homeliest guy in our pledge class. None of the sorority sisters wanted to kiss him. I felt sorry for him as they said it loudly so all of us could hear. They finally got a tube of lipstick and painted lips on his cheek. We left and went back to the frat house.

All the way back I thought "I wish instead the note had said they had to dress me as a girl and force me to walk back to the frat house". This was strange because I didn't feel I was pretty dressed as a girl and if I had to walk across campus someone would surely see me and probably laugh at me which was what I feared the most. The only saving grace would have been the fact that I would have a cover—that it was a fraternity pledge requirement that I walk across campus dressed as a girl. Again the thought of being forced to be a girl excited me.

We all made it through the pledging process and became frat brothers. Shortly thereafter I moved from the dorm into the frat house which was located in an old house on Bogue Street that bordered the Red Cedar River. I got my own room which was really nice as it had a lock. So needless to say, I continued to cross dress in the privacy of my room. When I moved there I was just barely passing my classes. I guess they okayed me as a frat brother because they liked me and not because of my GPA.

Everyone knows that an integral part of frat life is drinking. Both my parents drank at home. Daddy had a heart problem and the doctor prescribed one drink each night – 1 jigger (8 oz.) of bourbon in a 16 oz.

glass of water. It was diluted down so much that he never got drunk. Mom had one drink each night with him except her jigger of bourbon was in a 16 oz. glass of coke. She never got drunk either. Since both of my parents were able to drink responsibly and were never abusive to me or each other, I thought I could drink responsibly too. Besides, I wanted to belong and drinking was expected. So I learned to drink beer. It tasted awful until I learned to pour it down my throat and not taste it. In fact, I learned to drink it *too* well. I went to drinking parties every weekend and always missed my 8 o'clock calculus class because I had a hangover. My grades plummeted even more.

My drinking made me feel like I belonged but I still wasn't happy. I realized more and more that the only time I was really happy was when I was dressed like a woman. I believe now that I joined the fraternity for two reasons: (1) to be in an environment that would make a man out of me and (2) it allowed me to live where it was acceptable to drink to excess and that allowed me to drown my fears of wanting to be a woman. However the alcohol didn't drown my sorrows, it just dulled the pain for a while but it came back when I sobered up.

The next year, while at the fraternity, they had another Miss Red Cedar Pageant. Since Phi Sigma Kappa was also on the Red Cedar River, we were asked to send a participant. I had another chance. In fact, I was asked. Once again part of me wanted to go. I wanted to say yes but my fears again got the best of me. I said no and proceeded to go to my room, shut and lock the door, and cried. I remember asking myself again – why wasn't I born a girl? Was God up in heaven laughing at me? I remember crying this time for a long time. I told myself that I wished I had died with the other babies Mom lost. The struggle between who I really was and who I knew I should be was becoming unbearable.

I tried to date while at the fraternity. I had two girlfriends. They both were very nice to me. I even went to meet the parents of one of my girlfriends, Sandy, upon her request. Her parents were also very nice but deep inside I just didn't feel right. Sandy didn't drink so we only went on non-drinking dates like to the movies. I was always a gentleman with Sandy and I treated her like a lady. Actually I treated her like I would have liked to be treated if I were a lady. She was very sweet and pretty but I just wasn't physically attracted to her.

The other girl, Adrian, liked to drink and she frequently went with me to drinking parties. One such party was an off campus pledge party that was designated a Roman Toga Party. All our parties were off campus as it was against school policy to allow drinking on campus. When we got there, the actives were dressed like Romans, wearing togas, and the drink was not beer but purple passion (vodka and grape juice). They started the drinks with 1 oz. of vodka and filling the rest of the 16 oz. glass with grape juice. When that was gone, the next drink was half vodka and half grape juice. I got pretty plastered after two drinks.

I was in the corner of one of the rooms making out with Adrian when, while giving her a deep passionate French kiss, it hit like lightning. I gagged and threw up all over her – in her mouth, on her face, and on her clothes. It hit so fast I didn't have time to draw away. Of course it covered me too. She ran crying into the bathroom to clean up. I went into another bathroom and cleaned up. After we had cleaned up as best as we could, she turned to me and told me strongly, "You're walking me home NOW. Get someone to drive your car back to the frat house." I said, "Yes ma'am".

I proceeded to walk her back to her dorm which was 1.5 miles away. During that walk she proceeded to chew me up, spit me out, and chewed me up some more. She clearly told me that I was on 'the fast track' to become an alcoholic. She said, "You are sick. I used to like you but I don't like the person you have become. The alcohol has made you selfish and I don't like being with you anymore. Putting me aside, you need to take a long hard look at yourself because if you keep going the way you are now, you are going to be an alcoholic and will not only destroy all your relationships but you will also destroy yourself." It hurt to hear it but I knew I deserved everything she said to me. No one at the frat house had been so bold as to tell me that I was drinking too much. No surprise there as that was what was expected of everyone. I got her home and then I proceeded to walk back to the frat house which was on the other side of campus.

When I got into my room I looked in the mirror and it scared the crap out of me. I saw death looking back at me. For the first time I saw what I was becoming and I decided then and there I was going to stop drinking. If I didn't, I knew it would end up killing me. I fell on my knees and I cried to God to take my desire for alcohol away. I told Him I didn't want it anymore. I prayed and cried all night. I had never prayed so hard in all my life. I prayed so hard that I finally passed out on the floor from exhaustion. In the morning when I awoke and looked in the mirror, I saw a new person. God took the desire of alcohol away from me and I didn't desire it anymore. Halleluiah! Prior to that night, at my peak of drinking, I was drinking two 16 oz.

six packs of malt liquor a night and chasing it with a pint of bourbon. That all stopped. In fact, I quit going to frat drinking parties on the weekends. Instead I went to the Library and studied. Imagine that!

I had been drinking that hard for about three months before this life changing party. I didn't ever plan on drinking that much but, as is true with alcohol and alcoholics, one thing leads to another and before you know it you're hooked. It was real easy for me to get hooked though as my drinking was one of the ways I coped with all the pain in my life. I hated my body and wanted to be a woman. The last girl I had a relationship with in High School dumped me because she said she didn't have time for me. I was failing my classes (I had a 1.7 GPA). I gave up on engineering school and tried to get into the vet school and was turned down there. The list seemed endless. It seemed that everything I tried to do ended up in failure. So alcohol helped to dull the pain.

I know now that, among other things, my drinking was destroying my body. I am amazed that my liver has not given out by now. But God took away my desire to drink and I also believe He healed all the damage I had done to my liver. He obviously is not through with me yet. I give Him all the honor and praise! Adrian and I never dated again after that night. I really don't blame her. Once you throw up in a girl's mouth that is pretty much a deal breaker. But she had a hand in saving my life. Without her harsh scolding I don't believe I would have been open to God's healing of my desire to drink.

Trying to fill a void or escape the pain with alcohol or any other drug DOES NOT WORK. It is only a temporary fix at best. When you awake from it, you still have your problems plus others including headaches to go along with the heartaches you tried to cover. You still feel empty. After every time I drank and sobered up I still wanted to be a girl and I still felt the fear of discovery and rejection. Nothing changed by drinking.

This whole episode not only opened the door for me to stop drinking but it also made me realize that I didn't belong in the fraternity. Yes, I had friends but those were basically drinking friends. I realized I really didn't have anything in common with the guys there other than drinking. I was there only because I believed that being there was a means to make me a man. It didn't work. I wasn't any more of a man when I left than when I joined. I realized it was too dangerous to stay. The temptation to drink again was constantly there especially when there were drinking parties every weekend. So I decided to leave.

Not only did I leave the frat house but I left Michigan State University totally in 1969. My GPA was 1.7. I had failed most of my classes and with my current GPA it was going to be hard to get into any other college. I was going to have to go to a small college, study hard and start over so I could prove myself. Only then would I have any hope of getting into another university.

I had failed college and I had failed myself. Instead of being better off than when I started, I clearly was worse off. I was a failure to my Daddy who paid for my college education. I was a failure to my advisor as I basically flunked out. I was a failure to my fraternity brothers as my GPA was so bad it poorly reflected back on their image as an educational fraternity.

But worst of all I felt I failed God as the man he created. Even though I felt like a woman inside, God had anatomically made me a man. And I felt like I failed myself. I was confused now more than ever.

Chapter 4
Be a Man—The First Try

Since I had failed at Michigan State University, I lost my college deferment and became eligible for the Vietnam War draft. I was not a supporter of the war and really didn't want to go. I wasn't a radical demonstrator, yelling obscenities about our President and Congress for sending our best young men over to a foreign country to fight and die in a war that was purely political. Even though I had strong feelings about the war, if called I decided I would serve in whatever way I could outside of combat. I was pretty sure that if I went over there to fight I would be killed. I was a pacifist at heart and didn't have the killer instinct to stay alive in combat. I knew that if a situation occurred during battle where it meant my life or someone else's, I would die as I could never kill anyone for any reason.

After I left Michigan State, I had to make some decisions as to where I would live. I knew that I didn't want to live at home as Mom and I were not getting along at all. Anytime we were in the same room sparks would fly. During my middle through late teen years we fought continually. We seemed to misunderstand each other all the time. No matter what we said or how we said it, the other would get mad. Poor Daddy had to mediate between us all the time. To this day I don't understand exactly why we fought. Maybe subconsciously, I was reacting to fears about my gender dysphoria and took it out on

Mom. At the time I blamed Mom's mental health issues for her behavior but now I don't think it was her at all. I think it was me. I was just unhappy with life and she happened to receive the blunt of all my anger. So to keep peace in the family I wanted to get back into college but that was going to be hard since my GPA was so low.

I decided to apply anyway to a number of community colleges in the area. Surprisingly I was accepted at a small Christian college, Michigan Christian College in Rochester, Michigan near home. They said they were willing to give me a try. I started the spring semester of 1969 and did much better academically not being at the fraternity and not drinking.

I didn't declare a major as I didn't know what I wanted to do with my life. I ended up taking a current events class that was okay but I didn't keep up with reading the paper like I needed to in order to do well so I got a C. I also took Economics which I hated yet got a B; General Inorganic Chemistry which was a good class and I got a B; a religion class, the Epistles of Paul which was also good and I got a B; American Government in which I got an easy A as I loved history; and a fun class, Bowling, which I excelled in because I was a good bowler, another easy A. The point is that I had a good semester and the best grades I had ever got in college – an overall average of 3.13 for the semester.

Not only did my stay at Michigan Christian College help boost my GPA and my belief in my ability to do well in college, but it also opened the door to a very special relationship. While there I met a woman named Shirley Barker. She was in a few of my classes and I liked being around her. We hit it off really well. We spent a good bit of time outside of class together and after a couple months I proposed marriage to her. I loved her, as much as I knew what love was, and was hopeful that our impending marriage would solve two problems: I would keep myself from living at home and fighting with Mom and maybe Shirley could make a man out of me. She was overjoyed when I proposed and said 'yes'. We decided to get married in September, giving us plenty of time to plan the wedding and for me to get to know her family.

I attended church with Shirley and her family in Birmingham, Michigan for the six months prior to our wedding and spent time with her family. I had hoped that spending time with the family would make them feel more comfortable when I announced that Shirley and I wanted to get married. I definitely did not succeed at doing what I had hoped.

When I announced to her parents our intentions to be married, I didn't ask them. I told them. Basically, I told them we were getting married with or without their blessing. Looking back I think my attitude and statements were very immature. I think I so desperately wanted to be a man that I wasn't going to let anyone change my mind or delay it. In my eagerness to get married I had reacted to the whole situation like a bull in a china shop. My lack of sensitivity cost me their trust for the entire seven years that I was married to Shirley. Interestingly, Shirley didn't pull me off to one side and try to stop my careless and insensitive approach. I never asked her why she let me do it but I suspect she was anxious to get married and get away from home as well and didn't want them to talk her out of it.

The wedding was September 12, 1969 at her church, Birmingham Church of Christ. It was simple and nice with the reception at the church. Shirley looked beautiful and her wedding dress was the most beautiful dress I had ever seen. When I saw her in it, I remember part of me longed to be the one wearing it—no surprise there. As a gift, a friend from Shirley's family gave us our honeymoon night at the Ponchartrain Hotel in downtown Detroit. The Ponchartrain Hotel was one of the most prestigious hotels in Detroit at the time so we felt really blessed to be able to spend our honeymoon there. It was definitely the ritziest hotel I had ever stayed in. We really enjoyed it with its spectacular view across the Detroit River as we were on the 23rd floor.

We knew we both needed to finish college and Michigan Christian College was a two year college. We both applied to Olivet College in Olivet, Michigan and were accepted to start in the summer of 1969. Shirley had two years at MCC but I ended up with only one semester there.

Olivet was a quaint little town located 27 miles west of East Lansing. The whole life of the town centered on the college. The college was founded and supported by the Congregational Church.

The college was on both sides of Main Street on the north end of town. On the left side was the old stone Library which I loved to visit. I felt like I was walking back in history every time I walked through the doors. The next building, set back a little from the road, was the classroom building. It was modern with a metal front. All the classrooms were on one floor and had modern facilities and equipment. Across the perpendicular street coming to the classroom building, was the one fraternity and sorority at the college.

They were in neat old houses but I stayed away from the fraternity the whole time I was at Olivet because of my prior experiences at Michigan

State University. Across Main Street from the classroom buildings was the Student Union. It also was a modern building with the Union meeting room on the first floor and the bookstore/grill in the basement. Back toward town on the same side of the road was the college administration building. This building was probably 20 years old compared to the classroom and Student Union Buildings. So the campus was a nice mix of the old and the new.

At registration we both decided to declare ourselves as Biology majors. We both loved Biology and felt that fit our strengths the best. Besides there were a multitude of disciplines in Biology you could pursue for a profession. We wound up being in each other's classes because we were both Biology majors in the same year in the program. That worked out really well as we studied together and benefited from each other's strengths. We both did very well academically while we were there. There was no student housing on campus so we had to find a place to live in town. We ended up living in two different homes during our time there.

One was an old stagecoach hotel built during the 1880's. We lived there for about a year. All the rooms were really small and I remember the floor was so slanted that all the dirt dust balls would roll to one side of the apartment. While we lived there we decided to go the local dog pound and adopt a dog.

When we went into the kennels we were overwhelmed with all the dogs there. They all were excited to see us and 'put their best paw forward' to get our attention. We couldn't decide on which dog to choose. Then I noticed a small Golden Retriever back in the corner of the kennel. He sat there looking lonely and dejected. He was holding his head down like he was ashamed to be there. I fell in love with him and told Shirley that was the dog I wanted. We got him, named him Buttons, even though most of the time we both called him Mr. B.

He ended up being the best dog I have ever had. He was devoted and so loving. I would take him with me wherever I went other than school. We were best buddies. After Shirley and I broke up he went to live with her parents and lived to the ripe old age of 16. In his later years his arthritis got so bad that her dad would have to carry him outside to pee and carry him back. They loved him too and it was very hard for them when they had to put him down. His arthritis eventually got so bad that he would cry all night from pain and they just couldn't stand for him to hurt so badly. I miss him a lot.

We stayed at the old stagecoach hotel for a year and then in 1971 we moved across the street to a home which we rented for the remaining year we were at the college. We felt so lucky to be able to get such a nice home to rent. It was fortuitous that we needed a place and met the kids of the old woman who owned the home.

It seems the kids of the woman who owned the home had to put their mom in a nursing home and needed someone to rent it to. It was a very nice home and we enjoyed our stay there. The only problem we had with the place was that it had a lot of knick knacks (which is common with older ladies) and they made us feel uncomfortable as we were always afraid we would break one. Fortunately we were careful and never broke anything.

During the entire time we were at Olivet College I struggled with cross dressing. I did it every time I had an opportunity when Shirley wasn't home. Shirley didn't know until one day when we decided to play strip poker. She hadn't played it before so I gladly taught her. We had fun until I suggested a modification. Instead of ending the game when one of us had taken all our clothes off, as we continued each of us was required to put on a piece of the other's clothes every time we lost a hand. In other words, she would put on my clothes and I would put on her clothes. She agreed and it was great fun except she noticed I was having too much fun. I think that was the first time Shirley realized that maybe I had a problem. From that day forward, she looked at me differently, a lot of times with a suspicious look like she was trying to figure out if there was something wrong with me.

One morning before Shirley left for school, the desire to dress was so strong that I got the shakes. Shirley noticed and asked me what was wrong. I told her I needed to put on some lipstick. She looked at me with a quizzical look but agreed to get her tube of lipstick. She said if I was going to wear it though she had to put it on me. I agreed and she put it on me. When she put it on me, I immediately quit shaking. She looked at me strangely (and rightly so), said goodbye, and left. Obviously we didn't kiss as I was wearing wet lipstick. I left the lipstick on until I had to leave for school about a half hour later at which time I took it off with Kleenex.

The desire to cross dress was getting stronger and stronger. It had now begun to affect my ability to cope with life in general. It was controlling me. It was what I thought of when I woke up and what I thought of all day.

Since I failed to get into vet school at Michigan State, I decided to try classes in different disciples in zoology. Maybe I could find a discipline that I could do as a profession. The first classes I took included Comparative Anatomy, Ornithology, and Mammalogy.

I really enjoyed the Ornithology class, which is the study of birds. Birds are not only wonderful singers but their plumages are so spectacular. Their behaviors are also quite unique, especially the mating behaviors of males with all their intricate dances. As an added bonus in the class I learned to identify many of the local birds I saw on campus. After I completed the class I thought that maybe I could be an ornithologist.

The Mammalogy class was neat too. It was great fun leaning about all the common mammals in Michigan. One of our class requirements was to skin a dead mammal, clean its skull, and prepare the skin for scientific study. Back then it wasn't against the law to pick up road kill like it is today so all of us students traveled the roads looking for dead animals to skin. I remember finding a nice skunk on the side of the road. I stopped the car and when I went to examine it I got a whiff of its strong pungent repellent. I decided against it and let it be. I didn't find anything else along the road except dogs and cats and I was not about to skin someone's pet.

I then looked along some paths in the woods and found a good dead vole. I skinned it, boiled its skull and prepared the skin as required. It was fun and I got the highest grade in the class. I also recall that one member of the class learned a hard lesson. Emmett also found a skunk along the road whose scent gland had not dispensed any fluid when it was hit. He took it home and proceeded to skin it.

You can probably guess what happened next. He broke the scent gland and it sprayed all over him. He had to get a friend to go and buy as much tomato juice they could find and he had to take a bath in it to neutralize the smell. What a mess. I felt sorry for him. And to add insult to injury, the skunk's skull was good but Emmitt didn't get a very good grade on his skin.

The Comparative Anatomy class was by far the most difficult of all the zoology classes I took. All three classes: Mammalogy, Ornithology, and Comparative Anatomy were taught by the same teacher, Dr. Richard Fleming. I really liked him so it wasn't the teacher. It was the subject. Anatomy was not my thing. In the class we had to learn the origins and insertions of about 50 muscles in the mammal's bodies. I struggled with memorizing all those muscles and their locations. I eventually passed the class with a lot of pain and tears and the worst part is that I don't remember anything about the class. I don't remember a single muscle name, its origin, or its insertion. One very important thing it taught me though was that I would not have been able to get through vet school. Vet students are required to know mammalian anatomy which includes muscles, their origins and their insertions. So I was glad I was embarrassed in this class instead of in vet school. I was definitely not going to be a vet or professor in comparative anatomy.

Then I decided to try an entomology class, the study of bugs. While at Michigan State I knew some students who took an entomology class and had to make a collection. They asked all their friends, me included, to give them bugs for their collection. I always thought that it would be neat to collect bugs for a collection but never took the class while there. Now was different. Now I wanted to find out what entomology was all about. Dr. Richard Fleming, who was the same professor for all the zoology classes I had taken, also taught this class which was a definite plus.

As soon as I started the class I fell in love with it. It was so natural for me. I had never taken a class like it before. I didn't have to study hardly at all and during the whole semester I only missed one test question which was a specimen identification in a lab test. As part of the class requirement, I had to make an insect collection (no surprise) and sort every specimen into taxonomic Families.

For those unfamiliar with a taxonomic Family let me explain here. There are over 350 species of mosquitoes in the United States. If you see a mosquito from California or from Michigan or from Florida or from Japan for that matter, side by side you wouldn't have any trouble telling that they were mosquitoes. They may be larger, smaller, or have different markings but they would still look like mosquitoes. A mosquito looks like a mosquito and nothing else. All mosquitoes belong to the same taxonomic Family – Culicidae.

So my collection had to be sorted into those groups of related species. To get an 'A' you had to have representatives of at least 60 Families. It just so happened the year I took the class in the winter quarter of 1970, Michigan had one of its longest winters on record. It became clear to Dr. Fleming that no one was going to get 60 Families of insects in the adult stage as there was still snow on the ground in the middle of May. So he agreed to let us dip in the streams and count immature specimens if we could identify them to Family. I was excited. I got a reinforced spaghetti strainer, bolted it to a sawed off broom handle, dug a hole in the ice, and dipped for immature insects. I was very successful. I was so successful that I was only one of two students to get the 60 Families and get an 'A' on the collection. During the process I collected my first treehoppers that changed my life.

My maternal grandmother lived in a cottage in St. Helen, Michigan. She was surrounded by woods and flowering plants, the perfect habitat for insect collecting. One day while there collecting for my class, I heard a loud snap. I looked down and on my shirt were two of the most fascinating insects I had ever seen. They were brightly colored and just so cool. I wasn't sure what Family they were but I definitely wanted to add them to my collection so I grabbed both of them, killed them, and mounted them for the collection. I know it may sound cruel to kill innocent bugs but they multiply so rapidly that it isn't going to hurt the population of most species if you collect a few for a scientific study. I always, and to this day, make it a practice not to collect any more than I need to for whatever project I am doing.

Upon keying them to Family I found they belonged to the Family Membracidae, commonly called treehoppers. They are small sap sucking insects that come in many various shapes and colors. That was the beginning of a love affair with treehoppers that has lasted for 40+ years. And, yes, I still have those two specimens in my collection. Every time I see them I am reminded, with amazement and joy, of how these two small insects changed my life. I am now one of 14 world authorities on treehoppers, doing identifications and descriptions of new undescribed species from all over the world. Even as my vocation later changed, my love affair with treehoppers remained, with me continuing to collect them and learn about them on my own.

As I stated earlier, I excelled in my entomology class. Along with Tom Bowling, we ended up getting the highest grade in the class. Dr. Fleming strongly encouraged both of us to pursue graduate school and the profession of entomology. We both agreed and knew then that we wanted to study bugs for the rest of our life.

I knew I loved animals, especially bugs, but I also knew I still loved animals and medicine together. I asked Dr. Fleming if there was some way I could combine the bugs and medicine. He said there was a discipline of entomology called Medical and Veterinary Entomology that studied the control of diseases spread to man and animals through the bites of various arthropods (insects, mites, and ticks). I decided that was what I wanted to study in graduate school. I wanted to get a Masters Degree in Medical and Veterinary Entomology. For the first time, in a long time, I felt good about what was happening in my life.

Before graduating from Olivet College, I decided to check out the Medical Entomology research that was being done at both North Carolina State University and the University of Georgia.

I first visited the entomology department at North Carolina State University in Raleigh, North Carolina. Dr. Axtell was doing research on the affects of Hypelates eye gnats on golfers in North Carolina and means of controlling them when they became a nuisance. Even though his program was good research, it just didn't excite me. I wanted something with more punch.

So I next went to the University of Georgia. There I met Dr. A. B. Weathersby who was doing potentially life changing research on natural immunity of mosquitoes to malaria.

He had found that not all species of mosquitoes could successfully transmit malaria when they became infected after feeding on an infected host. The susceptible mosquito species, as he called them, would die from the malaria parasite that was in the blood meal. But the other species of mosquitoes which he called refractory species would not die. The parasite would not kill them. Instead the parasite would live within the refractory species, complete their life cycle, multiply, and be transmitted during their next blood meal to another host.

Dr. Weathersby's research was trying to find out what was in the refractory mosquitoes' physiology that was giving it immunity to the malaria and if once he found it, he hoped it could be used in a vaccine to protect humans from malaria. Millions of people die every year from malaria so the potential significance was great. It was a no brainer. I wanted to be a part of this potential life changing research.

When Shirley and I moved to Georgia we settled in Watkinsville, outside of Athens, renting a home there. It was an adequate home but we had trouble with the landlord about keeping the mold and mildew off the walls. The walls would be covered after every hard rain. That was especially important as Shirley and I talked about having children. Shirley wanted a child to fulfill her natural mothering instinct and I wanted a child to make a man out of me. I hoped, as I had hoped with other things, that if I fathered a child that it would convince my mind that I was a man. I was not a good lover but I guess my persistence paid off as while we were living in Watkinsville, Shirley became pregnant with our first son, David (Davy).

Because my assistantship paid only $200 a month, I couldn't afford standard prenatal care for Shirley. I went out and got a part-time job as a Technical Advisor to a local pest control company to assist our financial needs.

Working for this company, Boland Bonded Pest Control, was a wonderful opportunity to get my feet wet as a professional entomologist. As Technical Advisor, I was responsible for training and going out to each pest control operator's difficult accounts and help them get the problems under control.

I have always enjoyed teaching so I loved the training part of the job the best. I had a pretty large personal insect collection which I used during the training sessions. The men loved learning which also added to the fun. The founder and owner, Mr. Boland, liked what he heard too and ordered a cabinet, drawers, unit trays, and pins so I could build a reference teaching collection of insect pests to assist in training.

Since I had not been involved in professional termite control, I was told to go out on accounts with the termite salesmen and learn how they pitched a job. We had the top termite salesman in the state working in our office so it was logical that I should go out with him when he sold a job. I was looking forward to seeing him work his magic. I soon got the opportunity.

When we did our free termite inspection I saw that the homeowner did not have termites. So afterward I expected the salesman to tell them that they didn't have termites and recommend that we do a free pest inspection to be sure they didn't have any other pest problems. The salesman did tell the homeowner that he did not have termites but he also told him he had a bad infestation of brick bugs. He showed him breaks in the brick mortar and holes in the bricks and told him that soon his house would fall down if he didn't get a contract with us to control his brick bugs.

Now, as a professional entomologist, I knew that there was no such thing as brick bugs. I also knew that the breaks in the brick mortar were caused by air bubbles that formed when the brick was laid, not by any bug. I pulled the salesman off to the corner away from the homeowner and told him that there are not any bugs that feed on brick. He said to me, "I know that. You know that. But the homeowner doesn't know that and I plan on making a sale here." When he went back to the homeowner he pressed the seriousness of the brick bugs destroying their home to the point of bringing the woman of the house to tears. I was really having a hard time with this whole thing. Because I was new I didn't say anything more. I let him make the sale and told myself that I was going to talk to the owner of the company when I got back to the office.

But before I could see Mr. Boland, my supervisor grabbed me, bragging about how the salesman sold a job to control brick bugs. I told him that I did not agree with lying. He turned to me and said, "You will agree with it and sign off on the contract or you're fired." I told him, "You can't fire me because I quit." I turned and left his office.

The next day the owner called me and wanted to know why I quit. I told him because my supervisor wanted me to lie and tell a customer that they had brick bugs. The owner was also an entomologist and knew better. He told me he wanted me to come back but I said I couldn't because I would be working under my supervisor and he would fire me because I challenged his authority. I thanked Mr. Boland for allowing me to work for him but I never returned. I know that not all pest control companies are corrupt. Mr. Boland was not corrupt but his head of pest control sales was.

A few months later I found out from a friend that the head of pest control was arrested and put in jail for embezzlement of company money. It appears that not only did he lie to customers but he was also stealing from the company.

After I quit I went to my college advisor and told him the predicament I was in. He went to the chair of the department and before I knew it I had been awarded a fellowship to finish my Master's degree. In other words, I did not have to work anymore while I was in my program. I was being paid to focus on my classes and to learn. That was definitely much better. My heart told me I did well by quitting. By doing what was right I ended up better than I was before. God definitely takes care of those who do what is right.

Even though I had a good paying fellowship, it still wasn't enough for regular prenatal care. So my poverty income qualified us for prenatal care at the Clarke County Health Clinic. That care allowed us to have free prenatal care and delivery of the baby for only $25 if there were no complications.

We signed up and all of Shirley's prenatal care was normal. We went to husband coached childbirth classes so I could be there to support her and see the birth of our child. Interestingly, as I watched the mothers-to-be go through 'pant blow' exercises I longed inside to be able to give birth. Giving birth, to me, is the greatest gift a woman can experience, being able to carry and bring life into the world. Inwardly, I wanted to experience that and to be a mom. Even though I wasn't on any hormones, I had mothering instincts. Interesting but confusing as was most of my life.

As the day drew near, we both were getting excited. We kept telling each other "we are going to have a baby!" After 9 months, Shirley's water broke at 7:30pm on August 22, 1972. The best hospital in town was the Catholic hospital so I took her there.

When we got there they took her right in and put her in a room. The nurses came in regularly, checking on her progress. Her increase in dilation was normal. We thought everything was going okay. When the contractions came real close together we asked for a doctor. The nurses left to find one and didn't come back for a long time.

Shirley could feel the baby's head crowning at 3:00AM the next morning but her pelvis was too small to allow the head to come out. Finally some nuns came in and told us that there was no doctor available to deliver the baby. Both of the doctors on call at the hospital that night were trying to desperately save the life of a teenager who had blown part of his head off with a double barreled shotgun. The nuns didn't know how to deliver a baby so we had to wait until a doctor became available.

No doctor came in until 9:15AM. When he did come in he immediately took Shirley in for an X-ray. When he returned he told me what both Shirley and I surmised, that her pelvis was too small for her to deliver the baby. He said he would have to deliver the baby with forceps. He then turned to me and said, "I noticed that her care was under the County Health Department". I confirmed and said. "Yes. It is". He said he didn't deliver babies under the County Health Department so I would have to sign over to private practice. His fee to deliver a baby was $668. It was my choice. But if I didn't sign over to private practice both my wife and my baby would die as he was the only doctor left in the hospital. I had no choice and signed the consent. On top of his demand to go private practice, he didn't allow me in the delivery room as he didn't believe in husband coached childbirth. After the delivery Shirley told me that he did give her a saddle block so she could watch. Our first son, David Paul ("Davy") was born at 11:15am, August 23, 1972.

But it was clear very early after Davy was born that something was wrong with him. My Mom noticed it right away. She noticed that he was unable to hold his head up when he should have been able to. He also crawled crooked, dragging one leg. Shirley and I decided to take him to a Neurologist. They ran two sets of EKG's and said he was within the normal range just a little slow. They said to watch him and urged us to have him retested periodically. My Mom didn't buy it. She said there was something seriously wrong with him. She was right. Then one day his, and our, life changed forever.

We were at home one evening on the couch in the living room watching TV. Davy had crawled into the kitchen investigating. We turned to check on him and he seemed fine. While he was in the act of pulling himself up while holding onto a kitchen drawer handle, Shirley and I heard a moan. We turned just in time to see him have a grand mall seizure, fall, and wedge his head between the stove and kitchen sink. We both ran into the kitchen. I quickly grabbed the stove and moved it out and Shirley stood Davy up. He had burn marks on the side of his head where they had rubbed against both the stove and the side of the kitchen sink.

The next day we took him back to a neurologist. They ran an EKG again and determined that he was severely brain damaged. One minute he was normal but slow, the next he was severely brain damaged. Their diagnosis was that the oxygen deficiency from his delayed birth had killed part of his brain.

Shirley and I were devastated. We talked a lot about what we were going to do. Neither one of us knew anything about treating nor caring for a brain damaged child so we sought every avenue we could find for help.

The State of Georgia Mental Hospital said they would help take care of him for us but only under two conditions: (1) we could visit him only when they said we could and (2) we had to sign off on all rights to him including agreeing to let them use him as a guinea pig to test drugs. We unanimously agreed that we could not do that. While looking in a bookstore for some resource material, we found a book titled *"What to Do about Your Hyperactive and Brain Damaged Child"* by Drs. Doman and Delcatto. We read the cover with great interest. In it the authors talked about a new patterning program they developed for people who had suffered brain damage caused by accidents. The program taught the good part of the brain, through manipulation of body parts and visual stimuli, to do the functions that the damaged part of the brain used to do before the accident.

We both felt that a prayer had been answered. We unanimously agreed to try to get Davy enrolled in the program. We found a program center in Atlanta and applied. To our great delight he was accepted and we started it with hopes that it was going to be our salvation, allowing Davy to eventually be able to function in society.

To do the program required hundreds of volunteers to come in and do Davy's manual manipulation. Finding the volunteers was not the problem as there were plenty that wanted to help Davy. Scheduling them however was a nightmare for Shirley so she found someone who agreed to coordinate some 60 volunteers a week to come into our home to help Davy with his patterning program. She was wonderful and a great blessing. We could never have done it without her.

The volunteers came from all walks of life. We had doctors, nurses, social workers, and many high school teens. Despite Davy's mental condition, it was amazing to watch him not only touch, but change, the lives of the people who worked with him. Davy touched many lives but one case in particular sticks my mind.

A young teen came with his parents to volunteer. His parents told us in private that he had been a problem teen and they had tried everything to get him to change his attitude and become responsible but were not successful. They were at the end of their rope. When he came to work with Davy, a young child struggling to do simple things with such courage, this young man's heart was touched and his life changed forever. His parents told us after he left for college that working with Davy had shown him his selfishness and he decided to get a degree in Social Work and dedicate his life to help others like Davy.

Davy seemed to improve some, advancing to higher levels of programming, but the continual stress of working with him was taking its toll on Shirley though I didn't see it. I worked with Davy in the evening and on weekends as I worked and was in school during the day. Shirley however didn't get a break from it. She was there with him 24/7. The main way that I was able to cope with the stress from school, work, and Davy was to cross dress in private.

But it was getting increasingly hard to find a time when Shirley was not at the house working with Davy. So my cross dressing relief time was limited and because of that I was on edge. Shirley, of course, was on edge because of the stress of meeting Davy's needs. So we had problems with getting on each other's nerves. The only times I could cross dress was when Shirley would go get groceries and I would stay with Davy. I would cross dress for a short time while attending to a crying Davy who didn't like to be away from Shirley because he was nursing. I usually only did it for an hour, giving myself plenty of time to change back before Shirley returned. The cross dressing wasn't very satisfying but I was glad for what I could get.

I remember an incident while working on my Master's Degree that severely frightened me. Shirley and I attended a Church of Christ while I attended the university. It was a nice church but its conservative stance on women bothered me. Women were treated as second class citizens. They were not allowed to speak in church or Sunday school unless they were teaching children. The general conservative atmosphere coupled with my fear of being discovered consumed me. I was unable to eat or sleep.

I had a good friend at the church whose name was Reggie. He was a minister waiting for a church appointment. He had gone to seminary and was a compassionate leader. I really liked him and felt comfortable around him. My lack of sleep from fear of being discovered necessitated me to talk to someone and I decided to make an appointment to see him. I didn't know what I was going to tell him but I knew I needed to talk to someone.

When I came into his office at the church he told me to sit down. When he asked me what was bothering me I told him I couldn't sleep or eat as my conscience was bothering me. Out of the blue he said, "Are you a cross dresser?" I immediately broke down and bawled. I cried so hard my gut hurt. After I stopped crying, Reggie looked at me with compassionate eyes and said, "It's okay". I was carrying the fear that someone would know and my greatest fear was realized—he knew. I asked him how he knew and he said he sensed it. I wonder now if God didn't tell him.

Looking back I see that God was telling me that my feelings were okay and not to let them bother me as He loved me. But I didn't see it then. I just feared ridicule so much that I 'couldn't see the forest for the trees'. But now my secret was out. I asked myself, "What am I going to do now?" Reggie saw the fear in my face and reassured me, "Rest easy. Your secret is safe with me." He then took my hands and prayed with me. I don't remember what he said in the prayer but I do remember that when he was done my fear was gone, at least for that moment. Someone now knew and amazingly it was okay. But I then wondered if Reggie knew who else knew.

The cost of Davy's medical treatments was high (over $1,000 a month) and with my paltry assistantship, I became very discouraged. I kept asking myself, "What am I going to do?" It seemed like we couldn't keep up. I couldn't help but believe that my cross dressing was making God angry and all our hard times was His way of telling me to 'straighten up'. Then two events happened that made me wonder if my fear of God's displeasure with me was a figment of my imagination.

Mom and Daddy came to visit us one summer to see Davy when he was around two years old. A bad storm came up while they were with us and a tornado watch was issued. We kept watching the TV and saw that a tornado had been sited coming toward us in Athens. We decided to huddle with Davy under our big dining room table and wait out the storm. In a two bedroom apartment we didn't have many places to go.

We soon heard tornado sirens and knew a tornado was nearby. Instead of leaving and going to a shelter, we decided to stay under the table and pray. Within minutes we heard a loud sound like a train outside the apartment accompanied by high winds. We were sure that our apartment would be hit but the storm passed and we were spared.

After the all clear siren was sounded we went outside to check for damage. Our cars had tree branches and leaves on them but no bad damage. We looked on both sides of our apartment and found they were totally demolished by the storm. We all four looked at each other in amazement.

Amazingly the tornado had leveled the apartment on our left, jumped over our apartment and then leveled the apartment on our right. God had spared us. I wondered at the time why He would do that when I felt He was angry with me. But because He spared us, He must have plans for me and the rest of my family for the future. In other words, He wasn't done with us yet. So maybe God wasn't unhappy with my life after all. If He was, He could have ended my life then and there.

The second thing was our church's response to one of the times when Shirley and I didn't have enough money to pay Davy's bills. I don't remember telling the church we were short of money and neither did Shirley but somehow they found out and planned a surprise for us. My Sunday school class had a birthday party for one of our members and Shirley and I went. Toward the end of the celebration our teacher came out with a large branch of a tree stuck in a large pot of soil with bunches of silver dollars hanging on the branches. We thought the gift was for the member with the birthday but it was for us. The class members and members of our church had taken up a love offering for us. The teacher told us that he went to the bank, changed the money into silver dollars and individually tied them on the branches. I don't remember how much money was on that tree but I do remember it was enough, along with what little money we had, to pay Davy's medical bills that month.

What I remember most is that both Shirley and I cried when we received the gift as it was such a powerful outpouring of love for Davy. Again, God had saved us. I thought again that if God was unhappy with my life, why were we receiving these blessings?

I eventually finished my Master's Degree in June, 1973 and got a job in Atlanta with the Georgia Department of Human Resources, General Sanitation Unit. It was the reorganized old State Health Department. This was during the tenure of Jimmy Carter as governor of Georgia.

My main responsibility was to assist and train the sanitarians in the local county health departments. I got to travel to most of the 159 counties in Georgia and meet each of the sanitarians. While working for the General Sanitation Unit I wrote a training manual for the sanitarians on control of medically important insect pests and rodents and designed three brochures for the local health departments to put out to aid the public in preventing roach, rat, mice, and mosquito problems before they occurred. I loved going to work with the sanitarians in solving challenging issues involving insects and rats. On one such trip I was fortunate to be able to save a sanitarian's life.

It was in Helen, Georgia. The sanitarian called and said the public was complaining about mosquito problems in the local schools. He had gone and looked and couldn't find where the mosquitoes were breeding. I met him in Helen and went with him to the schools to look and I didn't see any obvious breeding source either. Then I asked him if there was a dump nearby. He said no but there was a creek. He had been having problems with people dumping there. I asked him to take me to it. When I got there I immediately found the source of the problem. There were a number of old tires and used washing machines along the bank of the creek filled with rain water. When we got near them we were 'ate up' with mosquitoes. We looked inside and there were thousands of mosquito wrigglers (larvae) and pupae in the water. We had found our source.

While standing there talking about what to do, we both heard some buzzing. The sanitarian looked down and saw that he had stepped into a yellow jacket nest. Hundreds were streaming up, running up his leg, and stinging him. He said to run. We turned and ran toward the truck, spinning, and slapping the yellow jackets off of each other as we ran up the hill. When we got to his truck he turned to me and said, "Listen to me carefully as I have something very important to tell you."

I turned to him and listened with horror on my face as I noticed his face starting to swell. He first asked if I could drive a stick shift and I said yes. Then he said, "I am hyper allergic to bee stings therefore I am going to pass out in just a few minutes. I don't have an epi pen in my truck so my life depends on you getting me to the hospital. I am going to quickly tell you the directions to the hospital." He proceeded to tell me the directions which I luckily wrote down as he told me because he passed out just as he finished. I drove as fast as I could to the hospital, hoping I would not caught by the police.

I got to the hospital with no problems, ran inside and told them there was a man in the truck, passed out and having an allergic reaction to multiple yellow jacket stings. They immediately ran out, got him out of the truck, and inside for treatment. Within 15 minutes the doctor came out and said, "Your friend is very lucky. You got him here just in time. He had 200 yellow jacket stings on his legs and back. I gave him an epi shot and he will be okay but he had less than 15 minutes left before he would have gone into shock and never recovered."

He then turned to me and asked me how I was feeling. All during this time I had not considered my own situation. My back was hurting bad and itching like crazy. He asked me if I was hyper allergic to stings and I said not that I knew of. I had been stung as a kid but always had a standard reaction. He then took me into an examination room and told me to remove my shirt and pants. He looked at my back and legs and said, "You have a lot of stings too – about 150. I'm going to give you an epi shot too. You will feel fine in about 30 minutes. In the meantime I want both of you to stay here in my office so we can watch your recovery in case there are any complications." We both recovered fine and the sanitarian got me back to my car. His wife was obviously overjoyed that her husband was okay. I thanked God that I was at the right place at the right time to be able to save his life.

I did well while working at the General Sanitation Unit but Davy's medical bills kept mounting and their cost exceeded the money I was making there. It became clear to both Shirley and I that I needed to get a better job so I could make more money. In order to do that I needed to go back to college and get a PhD so I would be able to get that better job. I applied at Michigan State University again, this time to graduate school. I was accepted into the PhD program in Entomology. We packed up and moved to Michigan in hopes of a better life for all of us. I looked forward to going back to college.

I have always liked the university atmosphere and being at Michigan State helped to ease some of my stress. I did well in my classes and enjoyed working on my scientific research for it allowed me to work on my beloved treehoppers.

For my thesis I decided to work on the immature stages of treehoppers. Little was known about them and at that time there were no identification keys even to genus. So my thesis specifically was to do a phylogenetic study of the United States genera using the immature stages. That is to say to look at the evolutionary relationship between the genera as expressed through the immature stage. This necessitated me to borrow as many specimens as possible from all the large museum collections where immatures were positively identified through adult associations. In other words, they were found at the same time, at the same location. For those genera, where positive identification of the immature stage was not known, I had to go into the field and find them. The genera that were lacking positive immature identification were in the Western United States so I applied and got accepted to study at the Southwestern Research Station in Portal, Arizona in the spring of 1978.

I was happy about my research and the planned field trip to Arizona but the more I buried myself into my research, the lonelier I became. I was still not happy with who I was inside. And things were getting worse at home. The only time I was truly happy was when I cross dressed and Shirley was becoming more and more disenchanted with married life.

I was becoming more and more disenchanted with life in general. I feared that she was falling out of love with me as we hardly ever made love anymore. So I decided that maybe another kid would fix it and finally make me a man. During a rare amorous moment we were able to successfully make love and Shirley conceived again. Her pregnancy went well with no problems and Andrew, our second son, was born June 25, 1976 in Lansing, Michigan. He was a beautiful baby. I was filled with joy as I finally got to be there and watch him being born. He was delivered through husband coached childbirth. I had trained to do it for Davy but was unable to be there as Shirley had complications and the doctor wouldn't allow me in the delivery room. I had renewed hope. Now everything will be okay. Shirley will be happy and having two kids surely will make me a man.

Boy was I fooling myself. Things didn't get better. In fact, things got worse. We met with the directors of the Patterning Center in Atlanta and they told us, after 4 years of faithfully doing the patterning program, that they didn't believe Davy would ever be normal. In fact, they didn't believe he would even make EMR (Educateable Mentally

Retarded). They initially thought he would make EMR and be able to work in the back of a fast food place like Kentucky Fried Chicken but now they said that will never happen. In other words, he will never improve much beyond where he is now. I looked at Shirley and I could tell that their announcement devastated her. She broke down and left the room. As I look back I think this was the breaking point in our relationship. She had wrapped her life up in Davy and now her hope was gone and soon she would find the only way she could cope was to get out away from it.

I noticed she started spending more and more time away from home in the evening, leaving me with Davy. Sometimes she didn't even come home. No matter how much I objected it didn't matter and that increased the stress on me. Davy was still dependent on Shirley so when she left he cried constantly. My hands were tied as he needed Shirley so I was not able to get him to stop no matter what I did. Those times totally broke me down. Andrew was nursing so she was okay with taking him with her when she left.

Both of us became more and more unhappy which led to arguing a lot. During one argument Shirley swung at me, trying to slap me in the face. I raised my arm to block her swing and she hit me pretty hard, bruising her arm. She then proceeded to an attorney and told him I hit her. She obviously thought I had hit her as she had the bruise on her arm to prove it. Then after interviewing both of us the attorney told her she didn't have a case. He told us we needed counseling. I agreed but Shirley didn't want to see a counselor. She wanted out.

I don't know why but Shirley finally agreed to go see a female counselor (I guess through a referral from a friend). She went to see her a couple times and appeared to like her. After she had gotten

Shirley's take on the problems, she said she wanted me to come in for a session alone. I agreed to go because I wanted to do all I could to save our marriage. I wasn't happy but I believed in the sanctity of marriage and that when I made the commitment at the altar to 'remain faithful in sickness and health till death do us part', I meant it. I went and she was nice, listened to my side of the story and said we would need to have further sessions. Then for a reason I can't remember, Shirley said she wasn't going back. Shirley's parents became angry as it seemed that Shirley had given up and wasn't trying. So they asked their pastor to come and talk to both of us.

We both knew him and agreed to meet with him. I hoped that he could help us but I think Shirley just met him to get her parents off her back. He came to our home and talked to us both together, trying hard to get both of us to make concessions and try to save our marriage. I told Shirley I would do whatever it took to save the marriage. I even made a list of things I would change. Again, all she could say was she wanted out.

While on a visit to Shirley's parents' home one weekend the realization of our imminent divorce hit me. I was so overcome I broke down and bawled. I believed that divorce was against God's will and that I would curse Shirley if we divorced. Then I started to think, "What is going to happen to Davy?" It was too much for me to bear. For the first time in my life I thought about committing suicide. All I could think about was how I had shamed my wife, how I had failed as a parent, how I had shamed Shirley's parents, and how I had shamed God. He surely couldn't love me anymore. So why live. I decided it would be best if I ended my despicable life.

I told Shirley one night while in bed of my plans to commit suicide and she said, "Ok. If that's what you want." That was not the answer I had hoped she would say. Even if she didn't love me anymore, I had hoped that she say something encouraging. At least she could have acknowledged that my life had value and urge me not to do it. But she didn't which confirmed in my mind that I was indeed a despicable creature and didn't deserve to live. So I decided to go ahead and make plans to commit suicide within the month.

Then one day, unexpectedly, when I came home from the university, Shirley changed the locks to the apartment and I couldn't get in. She also took the car somewhere and wouldn't tell me where. I had no place to go. I called an entomology buddy and told him I needed a place to crash as Shirley had changed the lock on my home. He gladly said I could sleep on the floor of his apartment that night in a sleeping bag.

The next day I called Shirley's Dad and told him what Shirley had done. He got real mad at her. He was a deacon in the Church of Christ and believed, like I did, in the sanctity of marriage and wanted her to try to work it out. Since he was paying for our car, he told her he was going to take the car from her because her actions were totally wrong. She told him she didn't care if he took the car away from her so he took it.

In the meantime, I got approved to stay in East Shaw Hall and had moved in. A few days later Shirley called me at the college and said, "I have put Davy out on the doorstep. I don't care if he lives or dies. If you want him, you need to come and get him." I couldn't believe she would do such a thing to her own child. I knew she was unhappy with me but why would she take it out on her own son? Now what am I going to do? Dormitory rules strictly forbid you from keeping kids in your rooms. I knew I had to go get Davy but I didn't know what I was going to do with him after I got him. I prayed for an answer and, as He always does, God answered.

I didn't know it at the time but I found out that a family in the church I was attending was licensed foster parents. And more remarkably they were licensed for 5 beds and they only had 4 foster children at the time. I talked to them and they gladly agreed to take Davy in to live with them until I could find a permanent foster home. Wow! I couldn't believe it. What a blessing! I immediately got in contact with Social Services and applied for permanent foster care for Davy. In the meantime, I picked up Davy and took him to their home.

No matter what we tried, it seemed that our marriage was doomed. It takes two to want to save it and Shirley made it clear many times that she wanted out. I was devastated. We went to a lawyer we knew in our church and he drew up the divorce papers. We filed and the hearing was September 12, 1976. I went but Shirley never showed up. Since Shirley's actions of leaving Davy on the doorstep was obviously not in his best interest, the judge gave me custody of Davy. Andy was 7 months old and nursing so the judge gave her custody of Andy. I made little money under my assistantship. I had left Boland Bonded Pest Control so that didn't enter into the equation so the judge said I didn't have to pay any alimony. I did have to pay child support for Andrew though which I dutifully paid every month until he turned 18.

I don't blame Shirley for any of her actions. She was under tremendous stress from giving her life to Davy. Consequently we grew apart and she did what she had to do to cope. The realization that Davy would never be normal enough to function in society was too much for her to handle. Her actions regarding Davy, I believe, were the result of a break down. I never believed that she stopped loving him. And my beliefs were confirmed a number of years later.

After Davy had been in a number of foster homes Shirley called one them and said she wanted to come and see Davy and be a part of his life again. The foster parents called me and asked what I wanted them to do. I told them to definitely welcome her and let her visit but just not to let her take him from the home. I was thrilled. I knew she loved him. Finally she had healed enough to invite him back into her life. He needed her in his life as much as she needed him. They made arrangements for her to come and visit and I talked with the foster parents later and they said everything went very well. Davy remembered her and enjoyed their time together.

As Davy's court appointed custodial parent I encouraged Shirley to continue to spend as much time as she wanted with Davy. Her presence in his life has been a tremendous blessing for him. Davy is now in a Developmental Center in NC and Shirley continues to visit him regularly. The staff says he truly enjoys her coming to visit especially their trips together to shop, eat, and to attend ball games. I am very comfortable with her love for him now and because of it I have now written her in my Will to get full custody of him at my death.

After the divorce was final, I realized that most of my failures in life were a result of my inability to cope with my cross dressing.

Yes, I had two beautiful kids but I had failed miserably as a husband and ruined a wonderful woman's life. I used Shirley. I had hoped that marriage and having kids would make a man out of me, causing me to stop cross dressing but it didn't. I was still cross dressing, probably more than before I got married. Cross dressing was a curse! I couldn't stop it and it was eating me up. Now I didn't know if I was a man or a woman. I didn't know if I was gay or straight. Nothing in life made any sense. I didn't even know if God loved me anymore. And was He going to curse me for all eternity for allowing my marriage to end? There are so many questions and no answers anywhere.

Chapter 5
Be a Man—The Second Try

The only thing in my life now that seemed to matter was continuing to work on my PhD and work with my beloved treehoppers. School became an obsession for me. I wanted it now more than ever. I told myself I had to salvage something from this tragedy. Even though I focused on school and was working with my beloved insects, I was empty and unhappy. I knew that the emptiness was because Shirley was gone. I missed her terribly. After 7 years of marriage I knew that I was empty without someone special in my life.

I also knew that the unhappiness was largely due to my struggle with having just divorced Shirley. I had always been taught throughout my life that divorce was a sin. I just couldn't reconcile in my mind, or in my heart that God could love me when I broke my commitment to Shirley to 'love her till death us do part". Even though she was as much responsible for the divorce as I was, I felt responsible for not making it work. Because of this burden of feeling the divorce was a sin, I felt uncomfortable going to church. I stopped going and I didn't know when I would ever go back. God was no longer an active part of my life. And without God, I was really empty.

I knew I was a 'people person' and I was only complete when I was around other people. Since the divorce I was alone and that intensified my loneliness. So I decided I had to find an avenue to meet people. In the dorm, East Shaw Hall, there were a number of European students who I befriended. I knew they had a European student group on campus and that they met at my dorm. As I started going to their meetings and hanging out with them, I found that part of my loneliness went away.

In September of 1977 the European students wanted to have a Wine Tasting Party. The premise of the party was to combine wine tasting with a dance that included a record DJ. Participants were given a card with a number on it when you entered the dance hall. Periodically the European hosts would stop the dance and hand out a small paper tasting cup with a number on the cup and a European wine sample in it. You were asked to drink it and decide if you liked it. If you did, you were told to remember the number of wine on the cup. At the end of the dance, after you had sampled 6 wines, you were asked to write the number associated with the wine you liked the best on a card with your name on it and put into a box. A card was then drawn from the box and the winner got a bottle of the wine they liked the best.

The European students rented a house about a mile off campus for the party. Most of the European students didn't have cars so they asked me if I would go around campus and pick up people who wanted to come to the party. I was happy to be able to help and agreed to pick up the students. I went to 4 dorms and picked up about 12 girls for the dance. It was during one of my dorm trips that I first met the girl who would become my second wife.

The last dorm I went to was West Shaw Hall (the girl's side of my dorm). I picked up the last three girls and proceeded to the party. After I dropped the last of the girls at the party I went to sit down and wait for the DJ to start a song. I wasn't a good dancer but thought that this might be good way to meet a girl who I could at least be friends with.

When the dance started I asked two different girls to dance the first two dances. Each of the girls were nice but no 'bells went off'. But the third girl was definitely different. She was tall and very pretty. We danced and surprisingly I really enjoyed it. She not only was very pretty but she had the most engaging laugh. When I heard her laugh it made my spirit feel good. We talked quite a bit and seemed to hit it off. I ended up spending the rest of the evening with her, talking and dancing most of the remaining dances together.

Before they announced the winner of the free bottle of wine, we looked at each other and didn't know which wine we liked the best. We just knew we hated the wine from Greece – we both thought it tasted like pine oil. Neither of us won the free bottle of wine but interestingly the winner chose the wine from Greece as their favorite. We both shook our heads and laughed. The dance was now over so I gathered the girls together from each dorm so I could take them home. I left the girls from West Shaw Hall till last since they were at my dorm. I noticed the girl that I had spent so much time with at the dance was also from West Shaw Hall.

I dropped her off and went back to my dorm. When I got inside my room I wanted to kick myself. I knew I was taken with the girl I had danced with but, in my stupidity, I forgot to ask her what her name was. I was determined to find out her name so I could see her again.

A couple days later I decided to go to the front desk at West Shaw Hall and ask the receptionist if she might know her.

When I met the receptionist I described the girl to her, including her wonderful laugh, and she knew her name right away. She told me her name was Pamela Moyer and also what room she was in. I think she could tell I was smitten with her so she was kind to me and told me the information I needed. I decided then and there that I had to see her again. But I was afraid she wouldn't want to see me again so I decided to trick her.

I went back to my room and ordered a pizza that was too large for me to eat alone. I had it delivered and after I got it, I called her and told her I had ordered a pizza, couldn't eat it all and that it would be a shame to throw it away. I then invited her to come to the common area and share it with me. The trick worked and she agreed. After we ate the pizza I asked her if she wanted to go for a walk. Again I was surprised when she said yes. I thought to myself, "This is all too good to be true. If I'm dreaming I don't want to wake up."

Our first 'real date' was at Red Lobster in East Lansing. Pam sat across from me and I remember not being able to take my eyes off her. She was the most beautiful woman I had ever seen. When she smiled and laughed, I melted. Pam saved our swizzle sticks from our sweet dinner drinks and kept them in our remembrance scrapbook as a reminder of what a great time we had. We continued to spend as much time together as we could when we weren't in classes.

We started walking on campus every night. On one walk across the center of campus, before I knew it, our hands touched and we were holding hands. Just like in the movie, "Sleepless in Seattle", it was like magic. After we locked fingers, I looked at her and she looked at me and both of us knew something special had just happened. We kept walking and talking.

I found out that she had come to Michigan State University for the Masters program to study microbiology. She graduated from Virginia Tech in Blacksburg, Virginia with honors and a major in Biology and minor in Chemistry. I was excited that she was a biologist and someone who had a passion for science like I did.

We continued holding hands and feeling totally comfortable with each other. I never dreamed I would feel this way after divorcing Shirley. We eventually came to the center of campus and stopped at a railroad crossing there. It just so happened that while we were there a train came by. While it was going by, I turned to Pam, she turned to me and we kissed. Both of us recalled feeling chills when we kissed. I probably felt chills when I kissed Shirley but I don't remember it. To this day I remember the kiss at the railroad tracks with Pam. It was one of those unforgettable kisses because of how it made me feel.

When the kiss was done we both acknowledged that our chemistries told us that we matched. Now I really was confused. I got chills kissing a girl but yet deep down I felt like a girl. What did that mean? Was I gay? I never thought of myself as gay but now I didn't know. All of these feeling didn't make sense. If I was truly a girl why wasn't I attracted to boys?

We continued to see each other after the infamous walk. We got together whenever we could. I even slept with her one night in her dorm room, together, on her couch. We snuggled and loved for our naked bodies to touch each other. We didn't have sex because both us were religious. She went to church and wanted to save it for marriage and I guess my Christian morals were still there even though I hadn't gone to church in a quite a while as I felt the same.

Every time we were together we held hands and kissed. Every time our hands touched and we kissed, the same good feeling was there and the same voice in my head asking why I liked it if I was a girl. I would go home totally confused – elated for being with Pam, but crying because I didn't understand my feelings. I knew I loved her and that I wanted to be with her forever. Was she the one who would finally make me realize that I was really a man? That question could only be answered later but now I decided I wanted more than anything in the world to be with her. So I decided to propose marriage to her.

Proposing marriage was not easy. I had been burned and part of me was leery of getting into another permanent relationship. Yet the part of me that loved Pam won out. I finally got up enough nerve and proposed at midnight, November 4, 1977 (November 5 actually). She never hesitated. She kissed me and said yes. When we started talking about a date, we both said we wanted to get married as soon as possible, like in January. Pam said she wished we could get married that soon but that she would need more time to plan the wedding. She was an only daughter and was sure her parents would want a nice church wedding.

She had decided that she didn't like her Master's program at Michigan State and was going to quit. She said that she would be happy to work and support me until I finished my degree. I was touched by her sacrifice for us. So we decided to wait until May 8, 1978. Pam reminded me that if we were getting married I needed to meet her parents. She said Christmas would be the perfect time.

So I agreed to go home with her to Newport News, Virginia over Christmas, 1977, to meet her family. I looked forward to sharing our exciting plans. But it was not meant to be a joyous occasion. We told them that we *were* getting married, not that we *wanted* to get married, and Pam's parents 'hit the roof'. I screwed up again when I told my bride's parents that I wanted to marry their daughter. Why didn't I learn from my first failure? They said "How dare you tell us you are getting married without our consent?" Her mother was livid (here we go again!). Then matters got worse.

She told Pam she disapproved of her marrying someone who was married before and especially someone who had kids. She told me, "Pam will never be first in your life because your children will always be first as they are blood". I told her that was not true but she didn't believe me. In fact, she never did believe me the entire 31 years Pam and I were together. I was never able to convince her of how much I loved her daughter. Anyway, what a mess! Definitely, this was not a good way to start a relationship with the in-laws.

The rest of the visit was strained because of the beginning and when we left to fly home it was apparent that Pam's Mom and Daddy did not approve of me. I guess I really don't blame them. I was obnoxious, presumptuous, and not considerate of their feelings for their one and only daughter.

After we got back to Michigan Pam and I sat down and talked about the visit. We both agreed that even though the visit went badly we still wanted to get married. So the question became how we were going to arrange the marriage. I knew I had to go to leave for Arizona to work on my research in March and would need to be there over the whole summer. Therefore I wouldn't be able to be there to help her. Pam understood that and we agreed that she would stay in Virginia and plan the wedding with her Mom while I went on to Arizona. I would then fly back to Newport News, Virginia, for the wedding on May 8, and after the honeymoon we would fly to Arizona together and remain there for the duration of my field research which was until September.

I left for Arizona in March of 1978, as planned, to start my research. I drove down with a college friend, Mike Evans, from East Lansing, Michigan to Portal, Arizona. There were a lot of horrendously long driving days but we were able to break it up by periodically stopping along the way to collect treehoppers. We finally got to Portal, Arizona three days after leaving Michigan.

The town of Portal was nestled at an opening at the base of two ranges of the Chiricahua Mountains in southeastern Arizona. On the map it was located in the southeastern most corner of Arizona with New Mexico on the east and Mexico on the south. To get there we traveled across western Texas through southern New Mexico into Arizona. All of this area of the country is nothing but hot, dry desert. It is so hot during the day that the sand temperature gets up to 125 degrees. So hot it would fry an egg.

The area of the Sonoran Desert where Portal was located was called the flats. It is an entomologists dream, teaming with insects, and spiders (including tarantulas, scorpions, and vinegaroons). After a sudden summer rainfall, the arroyos (the dry river beds) in the flats fill with water, flooding the desert. In a very short time the desert comes alive like at no other time. The flowers bloom all over the flats which brings out the insects. The insects are opportunists, visiting the flowers for pollen during the very short time they are in bloom. The beauty of the desert is beyond description during this time with all the purples, reds, and yellows. It's here that Portal is nestled and the Research Station is located.

The town of Portal itself is situated in the flats of the Sonoran Desert. It contained only one store and about 10 houses. The store was like an old timey general store and had a restaurant attached to one side. Pam and I ate there a number of times during our stay in 1978 and the food was really good. The town is so small that everyone knows everyone else, even the Research Station visitors. Since Pam and I stayed at the Research Station for 5 months (May through September), they came to know us real well and treated us like family. There was a road that ran through town and up one of the two ranges to the top of the mountain. About a mile up that road, on the left, was the Southwestern Research Station.

Mike and I stayed there from March until I left in early May for the wedding in Virginia. He was a great assistant, helping me with my research while Pam and her mom planned the wedding. Being at the Research Station was so much fun that both of us hated to leave. We flew out of Arizona (Mike for Michigan and me for Virginia) a week before the wedding. I felt bad that I didn't give Pam any input for the wedding but I couldn't since I was in Arizona. We wrote each other every day and I was able to give her a little input through my letters. I cherished every letter I got from Pam, as she told me she did mine. They were our lifeline to each other during this difficult time we were apart. When I got to Virginia I found out from Pam there were a few things left to do for the wedding so we went together to the local mall to shop.

I was amazed while we were at the mall as the local people there kept asking me what part of Virginia I was from. I had picked up on the Virginia accent in my speech so strongly that I sounded like I was born in Virginia. When we got back to her parents house and I spoke to her mom, her mom got angry with me. She thought I was mocking her accent. I told her that I wasn't and that I had picked it up naturally. She accepted my explanation, with some support from Pam, but I think she did so reluctantly. We finally got the last of the shopping done and it was time for the wedding.

May 8, 1978, our wedding day finally came. All was ready at Morrison United Methodist Church, Newport News, Virginia for us. I don't know about Pam but I was a nervous wreck. I had grown a beard while at the Research Station and looked much more mature than my 29 years. I met with the two fathers, Pam's Dad and my Dad, in the Pastor's study waiting for the signal to go into the sanctuary. I thought it would never come! Finally it did and we went into the sanctuary. I stood at the altar. Our only two attendants were already there – Pam's best female friend, Glenda Lovelace, her maid of honor, and my Dad, who was my best man. Finally the entrance music for the bride started (played by her oldest brother Michael), and I turned to look down the aisle. There I saw Pam coming, holding onto her youngest brother, David's, arm. Her Daddy then came out and proceeded to marry us as he was the minister of Morrison United Methodist Church.

Shirley was a beautiful bride but Pam was unbelievable. Seeing her in her simple eyelet gown I was mesmerized. As with most couples getting married, we couldn't keep our eyes off each other. The most touching part of the ceremony for me was when we lit the unity candle from the two altar candles on each side. As I lit the unity candle with Pam I distinctly remember feeling myself healed. I felt that all would inbe okay now as I was finally with my soul mate. The reception was in the church fellowship hall. It was very simple and for the first time I felt warmth from Pam's family.

We were very blessed and received many wonderful gifts. I got us a nice room for our honeymoon night stay at a hotel in Virginia Beach because Pam loves the ocean. The hotel was very nice and one of the most memorable things about our honeymoon was the morning after. We went out of the hotel and couldn't believe what we saw on the beach – thousands of horseshoe crabs mating. They were crawling all over each other, frantically mating. I remember thinking, "What an appropriate thing to see on a honeymoon – mating horseshoe crabs. Was Mother Nature trying to tell us something?" Unfortunately I had to get back to my research so we flew back to Arizona the day after we were married. I told Pam that I was not happy with only a one day honeymoon and promised her that during our time in Arizona I was going to take her on our 'real honeymoon.'

The Research Station was like an oasis in the desert. Most of the visitors were natural history researchers and birders. The grounds were rectangular, the facilities were located on all the sides and the center was open. Next to the road was a nice sized swimming pool for all the residents to cool off in after being out in the heat of the day. On the immediate right coming into the facility were four double occupancy cottages. Then going around to the left were four multi-room cottages. These were frequently used by large birding groups that were moving in and out all the time.

Next was the Director's cottage (Dr. Vince Roth, a spider taxonomist) and office. It was built from a log cabin kit and was really homey. Up the steps above the Director's office was the research lab. In the lab were cabinets and tables for working with arthropods and numerous hooks for holding black light traps. Then there was a creek on the left of the facility that was bordered on the near side by the caretaker and cook's cabin (the caretaker and cook happened to be husband and wife, Joe and Jenny) and the canteen. Joe took care of the grounds and maintenance while Jenny coordinated all the meals for the visitors. While we were there Pam worked for both Joe and Jenny to pay for her board and keep.

She worked very hard, sometimes being very sore as Joe would ask her to do hard work usually done by men, like assisting in concrete repair. She also cleaned some homes in town for some elderly citizens that were friends of the Research Station. She was paid and found that these were her best jobs. The people were very appreciative of her work and paid her well. While Pam was working at the Research Station or cleaning a home, I was out in the field searching for treehopper adult and immature associations for my research. I also was given a small stipend ($1,000) to collect as many insects as possible for the Michigan State University Insect Collection. It seemed at times that the University collecting became the focus of my collecting instead of my research.

Pam not only worked hard during the day but I asked her to help me collect and mount insects at night. We collected at the black lights and lab white lights almost every night. The diversity of insects was phenomenal. I was like a kid in a candy shop.

Poor Pam stayed up with me till late at night (midnight and beyond) many times just barely able to stand when we finally retired for the night. Her help, both working and helping me with collecting, was immeasurably important to the success of my research stay. I could not have done it without her. I told her many times of her importance but I didn't tell her enough as she became discouraged and overwhelmed with exhaustion. Looking back I can understand why. I don't know of any newly married wife who would like to do all the things she did for her husband right after she was married. It was so tough for her at times that she told me she wondered if she had done the right thing getting married to me.

We stayed in Arizona until the following September. In July I kept my promise and Pam and I took some time off for our real honeymoon. We drove up to the Grand Canyon and spent a few days. It was great to get away and be together. We really enjoyed the dramatic views and bird watching together.

We had difficulty with bonding as we were apart so much during the day. We made it though and came back to Michigan State in September, moving into a small apartment near campus (Cherry Lane Apartments).

All during the first years of our marriage I struggled with my gender identity. Pam was a beautiful woman but I couldn't keep an erection. I cross dressed when alone and dreamed about being a woman. I remember when I cross dressed I would look in the mirror, make gestures as a woman enticing a man and easily get an erection. Why couldn't I do it when lying next to my beautiful wife? Part of me hated these feelings as I loved my wife and I knew that my cross dressing feelings were wrong. Another part of me though enjoyed the feelings causing me to dream about becoming a complete woman. I would masturbate when I got an erection and then when I ejaculated I would cry. I would cry because I was afraid. I was caught in a trap and I didn't know how to get out.

I lost my funding for my thesis. My dissertation was too difficult a problem to solve in 4 years. So I ended up having to leave Michigan State AGAIN without a degree.

I applied for a job in Fort Myers, Florida at a Mosquito Control District and got the job. We moved to Florida and stayed there three years. Pam found work there as a chemist in a lab testing wastewater. But living there was difficult as the cost of living was so high. There basically were two classes of people there – the 'snow birds'; retired people from the North who were rich; and the working poor.

We were some of the very few middle class folks just barely making a living. Pam wasn't happy with her job and unfortunately the Mosquito Control job didn't work out.

Fort Myers Mosquito Control District was the most prestigious mosquito control district to work at in the United States. They had four DC-3 planes along with an airfield that they used to fog for the control of mosquitoes. They had the most modern and up to date equipment and a research lab. My job was to assist the head researcher with his field research. He had found that if he tethered a disk of monomolecular solidified oils to a stake in a pond, the melting oil film would provide an oil barrier on the surface of the water, clogging the siphon tubes of the immature mosquitoes causing them to suffocate and die. He had published a number of papers on the effective use of this control technique and I was excited to be a part of it.

During my time there he was asked to give a paper on his research at a conference. He asked me to maintain his research mosquito colony in the lab while he was gone. I had assisted in maintaining a mosquito lab colony while at University of Georgia as part of my part-time assistantship so I felt good about doing it. Pam even came with me and helped me. But for some unknown reason, part of the culture died.

When the head researcher returned he was very mad about the state of his colony. Because of the colony situation, he never trusted me again and I ended up having to leave after only being there about 6 months.

I did some odd jobs in plumbing and air conditioning for about a year but I knew that wasn't my calling. I had a wonderful, loving wife but I felt my life spiraling out of control. The desire to cross dress continued to grow each day. I couldn't wait to get home before Pam did from work and cross dress. To no fault of Pam's it was the main thing in my life that gave me joy.

We attended a very loving church, McGregor Church of Christ (now Gulf Coast Church of Christ), and had a number of friends in the church that we did things with and ate with. I taught Sunday school but felt uncomfortable with their theology. They believed that women were second class citizens and had to be quiet in church. They were allowed to teach the children but that was about it. Pam and I even taught the junior high youth for a while, taking them to Disney World once (pre Epcot Center). It was fun but we both decided that Florida wasn't for us.

We didn't know where we wanted to settle so Pam's parents offered for us to stay at their house in Poquoson, Virginia until we could find work and decide where we wanted to live. I wasn't happy about it because of how her parents felt about me but 'bit my lip' and agreed to do it for a short period of time. We lived there for 6 months while we looked for work, living out of our boxes which were stored in her parent's garage. Pam got a job with Black and Decker tool-company in purchasing and I got a job with Orkin Pest Control (Termite and

Pest Control Sales) in the Hampton Roads office. I quickly found out that sales are tough.

I loved the pest control part of it but I hated the sales end of it. Pest and Termite Control Operators had to drum up their own business. We had to make cold calls by phone or knock on doors in the morning, trying to get business. If we were lucky and got business, we did the service in the afternoon. We had to meet a monthly quota of sales or we went in the hole. The company covered us for one month but if we fell short again we were gone. Needless to say it was a lot of pressure. While working at Orkin there were three memorable pest control moments.

One involved a food store that had a rat problem. I went to the store, did an inspection, and found an alarming number of rat feces. By looking at the extent of the food damage and the number of feces, I determined that there was a huge population of rats visiting this food store. I knew that baited food would not work as they had all the food they needed in the store. So I decided to use liquid bait as rats have to drink when they feed. We had a license to use the most powerful liquid rat poison known at the time. No one at Orkin wanted to use it because it was so toxic. Just a little on your finger, if put in your mouth, would be enough to kill you. I knew how to use it safely so I volunteered to bait the store with it.

To use this highly toxic poison you have to put on heavy protective gear – gloves, mask, goggles, plastic pants, and boots. You also have to make a map that includes the location of every baited trap so you will be sure to pick each one up when done. In addition to all that, you have to place a note on the door of the store informing the community to stay out of the store as it contained highly toxic chemicals.

I put out about 25 baited traps, mapped their locations, and put a sign on the door of the store. I left them overnight. I knew the bait would work and it did. When I returned the next day there were dead rats all over the place. With protective gloves and mask, I went all over the store, picking up over 100 dead rats and placed them in bags that were going to be disposed of in a special hazardous waste facility. Just as I was about done the most horrifying thing happened.

As I looked behind the meat counter where they prepared the meat and fatback, I saw a rat. I initially thought it was dead but as I looked more closely I saw that it was still alive. It was sitting near one of the liquid bait traps so I knew it had taken a lethal dose of the bait and was dying. I stood still afraid to move as that might scare it and cause it to attack me. A bite from it could be deadly as it would put the rat poison in my blood.

I slowly moved over to an area where the store owner had some brooms leaning against the wall. I carefully grabbed two brooms. I held them by the broom part, extending their handles out in front of me. I stared at the rat. As I feared, the rat charged me in its final moments of life. I quickly took the two handles of the brooms and brought them down on the neck of the rat, crossing them as they met the rat, breaking its neck and killing it instantly as it fell at my feet.

Needless to say I was scared. I had never been charged by a rat before let alone one that could kill me with its bite.

I picked the rat up, put it in the bag with the others, and sealed the bag. My control program was successful. The store owner never had rats again as the baiting had killed all the members of the clan. And I had learned a very important lesson. I learned that sometimes the most dangerous enemy, in the pest control business, is not the poison. Sometimes it is the pest and all pests need to be treated with the utmost respect.

A second incident involved a termite inspection. I got a job to do a termite inspection in a home along the waterfront in Newport News. The home was old and had a very shallow crawl area. It was so shallow that in order to move in it, I had to pull myself along, face down, with my arms extended like I was swimming.

When I got to a place where I wanted to inspect the floor joists for termites, I had to take my screwdriver, dig a burrow wide enough for my head, and then turn over. I did this a number of times and found no termites. As I was about to leave, I looked up and to my horrifying surprise, were two adult copperheads, coiled and staring at me less than 5 feet away. I knew enough about snakes to know that if I moved quickly they would feel threatened and strike me in self defense. I decided the best thing to do was to slowly back up.

I knew I didn't want to take my eye off them and I had no way to move fast as the crawl area was so low. So I very slowly used my toes to pull myself backward toward the opening to the crawl area. Slowly I moved being sure I didn't scare the copperheads. After what seemed like an eternity, which probably was less than 10 minutes, I got to the opening and pulled myself out. I was never so happy to be out from under a house!

I informed the owners that they didn't have any termites but they had two copperheads under the house. They said they knew they had them under there. I said, "Why didn't you tell me before I went under the house?" They said they were afraid I wouldn't go if I knew they were there. Duh! I told them, yes, I would not have gone and they had no right to endanger my life by not telling me. Needless to say we lost their contract which I believe was a good thing.

A third incident that is strong on my memory involves everyone's most hated and despised bug, the roach. I was asked to help one of our pest control salesman with a very difficult roach account. When we pulled into one of the housing authority apartment complexes I knew I was going to be in for a challenge.

When the apartment door opened I was immediately blessed by the renter. She was a very sweet and kind elderly woman. She looked at me and started to cry. She said she had such a bad roach problem and didn't know what to do. She pleaded with me to help her. I looked in her cabinets and along her door frames and they were covered with roach feces. I told her she most certainly had a bad roach problem.

My fears were confirmed very shortly after we arrived as a dozen ran across my shoes (roaches aren't usually seen during the day unless they are real bad). I told her that we would need to fog her apartment and that she would have to throw away her food before the fogging and wash all her dishes and cupboards after the fogging. She was very happy to do it if it would get rid of the roaches. We set a date to come back in a couple of days.

When we went back, we told the renter she would have to leave. She did and then the pest control operator and I donned our masks, fired up the fogging machine and watch the incredible sight. In over 10 years of working in professional pest control I have never seen so many roaches. They were literally raining from the ceiling by the thousands. They were falling in our hair and down our clothes. Thank God we had masks on or they would have fallen into our mouths. I felt them all over my body and I wanted to rip my clothes off! When we were done, we swept the thousands of dead roaches off the floor and counter into bags. When we showed the bags of roaches to the renter she cried and then hugged us both. She was so happy. Her joy was well worth all we went through. However, when we left, we both radioed the office and told them we had to go home, shake out our clothes and shower. We felt awful. When we told him what had just happened he heartily agreed.

I became involved in Pam's Dad's church, Poquoson United Methodist, teaching adult Sunday school and really enjoyed it. But the whole time we lived with her parents I was unable to cross dress and it killed me. I became very irritable. We both were not happy as living out of boxes was getting old as well as living with her parents. We needed to be on our own. So we decided we had to leave Virginia.

Pam looked in the paper and found a job announcement for a microbiologist position in Gastonia, North Carolina.

She went and got an application, filled it out, and got a phone call interview. It was a position at the Poultry Division Lab in Gastonia, North Carolina. It required her to check egg samples from various egg suppliers across the country whose eggs were eventually going into dry mixes that the public would buy at the grocery store. It was a very important job but it would require her to work many weekends and some long days. She couldn't believe it but she got another call later and they said she was hired. Amazingly she didn't have to go anywhere for a face-to-face interview (is that good or what?). Apparently her exceptional scientific training and lab experience at Virginia Tech convinced them they had the right woman.

We then moved to NC and I requested a transfer from the Hampton Road Orkin office to the Charlotte, North Carolina office. I got a position in Termite sales, which I held for 6 months and then a position in Pest Control Sales. My sales numbers were good and I enjoyed my work except sales continued to be hard work.

Everything seemed to be going well except for my mother's death in March 1984 of cancer at the age of 56. Mom had struggled with cancer for over 4 years. It started as throat cancer (she smoked from the time she was 14) and then spread to her lungs, back, and finally to her brain. She was a very courageous woman, fighting hard to live. Mom loved Daddy so much that she did what most would consider impossible – she hand-picked Daddy's next wife.

While Mom was still able to sit up in bed, she called Daddy in to their bedroom and had him sit down next to her. She got the church directory and went page by page with Daddy, evaluating each woman's potential as Daddy's next wife. I remember Daddy telling me that he told her, "Helen, you're crazy. There is no way I'm going to marry any of those women." I know Daddy felt loyalty to Mom and didn't even want to think of her dying.

When she got to Ruthe's picture, Mom told Daddy that she would make the perfect wife to take care of him. She was a widow whose husband had died a few years before. Daddy just laughed and let Mom have her say. Little did he know that 2 years after Mom died Daddy would take Ruthe to the Big Boy after church for coffee and from that innocent meeting they would end up marrying each other 2 years later. It is hard to imagine, but Mom hand-picked Daddy's second wife that he loved dearly for the next 13 years of his life (Ruthe died in January 1999).

When Mom was nearing death, the family called me to come up to be with her in Michigan. I flew home a number of times but the time did not come. Since I am an only child I wanted to be there with Mom and reassure her of my love when she left this world but it was becoming a financial burden to keep flying home. Finally I told Daddy to be sure it was the end the next time he called. He called me at 3am and told me Mom had died. I was angry with him because I wanted to be there with her and I missed it. How could he not call me? Daddy told me she went quickly and there was no time for me to come home. He and Aunt Zelda (his sister) were there with her and held her hand as she went from this life into the next. Not being able to be there with Mom when she died 'ate me alive' for 2 years. I blamed myself, even though later I came to understand my lack of presence there was not my fault. Finally one weekend when I went up to Michigan to visit Daddy and Ruthe, I had Daddy take me to Mom's gravesite. I stood there at her grave and wailed for 30 minutes, asking Mom to forgive me for not being there when she died. Opening myself up finally let me forgive myself and feel inside that Mom had forgiven me long ago.

At Mom's funeral her minister asked me if I wanted to read her favorite scriptures. I agreed as I wanted to do it for Mom. We picked two of her favorite scriptures, one of which was in John 14:2-3 where Jesus says "Do not let your hearts be troubled. Trust in God, trust also in me. In my Father's house there are many rooms; if it were not so, I would have told you. I am going there to prepare a place for you. And if I go and prepare a place for you, I will come back and take you to be with me that you also may be where I am [NIV]".

Mom loved to have me and Daddy read her that scripture. It gave her so much comfort and for that matter I believe it gives most Christians comfort. It is comforting to know (1) that Jesus is preparing a place for us to be with Him and the Creator God forever; (2) that Jesus is coming back to earth to take us back with Him to that place that He has prepared for us; and (3) that Jesus doesn't want our hearts to be troubled. Boy, that last one touches me. My heart was so troubled. I was so afraid and confused. So when I read it I cried uncontrollably. Not only did it remind me of Mom, but it also spoke to me and my situation. That particular time is probably the first time that I cried regarding Mom at any time in my life. It wasn't that I didn't love Mom because I did but I just never felt real close to her. We had gone through some difficult times during my teen years and I guess I had put up walls that kept me from getting hurt again. But I cried at the funeral and really came to know how much I did love Mom.

Since I was the only one of her pregnancies to live and since she could never have any more, I never verbally told her of my gender identity problems. I loved her and never would do anything to hurt her (or Daddy). I kept it inside, hoping she would never truly know. When she died I believe she never truly knew. Mom was gentle and never finished high school so she looked at the world through innocent eyes. Any unusual mannerism she may have seen in me I feel sure she chose to ignore. I missed her after she died but now that I'm a woman I miss her more than ever. I wish I could have been able to know Mom as her daughter. I wish she were still here as I think she would have eventually accepted me as a woman and we could have had wonderful times together as two women.

I kept fighting the notion that I wasn't able to whip my cross dressing because I wasn't getting close enough to God. So I reasoned if I found a way to get close to God I would find my answer and the strength to be the man he created. All my attempts to live a life as my biological gender had not worked. I had definitely proven that I didn't have the answer within myself so the answer had to come from God. I prayed about it and decided to look into going into the ministry. I reasoned that maybe if I submitted myself to God, studied the scriptures hard, and prayed a lot, God would tell me the answer.

That had to be it. My problem must be that I trust myself too much to battle this demon and God was trying to tell me to surrender myself so He could expel it from me.

We had tried a Church of Christ when we first came to North Carolina but we didn't like it. Again they were too anti-women so we started attending the Methodist Church in Gastonia. We felt the love of Christ as soon as we walked in the door at Myers Memorial United Methodist. So it was an easy decision to start worshipping there.

I became very active at Myers Memorial. I recorded the services on tapes so they could be taken to the shut-ins, was a sub in my regular Sunday school class, taught the choir Sunday school class, and became a Certified Lay Speaker, filling in for pastors when they were sick or out of town. I was called on to guest preach pretty regularly and really enjoyed every opportunity I was asked to be in the pulpit.

I also became President of the Local United Methodist Men (UMM). During my time as President (1987-1988), our membership, participation, and budget grew. We honed our big fund raiser, Pig Pickin', where we raised the majority of our funds for our projects for the year. It was amazing to see how we were able, with all of the men pitching in, to cook, prepare, and serve BBQ chicken and Pork to hundreds of folks. Our BBQ was so good that folks became regulars and helped our projects by purchasing plates for many consecutive years.

I really enjoyed being president of UMM and made it known that I wanted to be the next Gastonia District President of the UMM. I applied and got accepted to go to the District Presidents Training Workshop in Hershey, Pennsylvania. I went, had a great time and within a few months became the new Gastonia District President of UMM. While President I divided the district into four areas and had coordinators reach out to the churches in each of their areas. This is so each UMM fellowship would have an experienced leader who lived nearby to assist them. I would try to visit each one of the 50+ fellowships at least once a year during the two years I was District President.

The Western North Carolina Conference President of UMM at the time saw leadership qualities in me and asked me to become one of his Conference Vice Presidents so I could be groomed to eventually become Conference President. I was honored and agreed to do so. I enjoyed being Vice President but felt my call was deeper. I prayed a lot about my call and strongly felt the call to ministry in the United Methodist Church. When I told the Conference President of my decision to pursue ministry after serving only one year he was disappointed but fully supported me.

After much prayer I talked with the District Superintendent for the Gastonia District at the time, Dr. Tom Sigmon, and he accepted my request to go through some evaluation classes to determine if I had the gifts and graces for ministry.

The classes were at the District office once a week for 6 weeks. During that period, I met personally, one on one, with the District Superintendant. We talked about my call to ministry, the gifts and graces (i.e. spiritual gifts and God given abilities to minister) needed for ministry and then testing to determine if I had the necessary gifts to be a local pastor of a congregation. The church did not recommend you to the Western North Carolina United Methodist Conference Office for a church until you had been appropriately tested. This filtered out people who wanted to be a pastor but would not be able to serve effectively in the United Methodist Church.

After attending classes for several weeks, Dr. Sigmon said he believed I did have the gifts and graces for ministry and recommended I put in an application to the Local Pastors School in Winston-Salem. I did and was accepted. Before going to Local Pastors School I had a very important spiritual awakening and strengthening.

I became active in a lunch Bible study group of fellow employees at my part-time job in Charlotte (Dun & Bradstreet Pension Services). A local Presbyterian church near our office was kind enough to let us meet there every week for our Bible Study. During our study we talked about gifts of the Spirit including speaking in tongues. As a Methodist I had been taught that speaking in tongues had ceased when the Bible was made available to everyone after Guttenberg's invention of the printing press in the 16th century. But deep down I wasn't so sure. The more we studied the more I became convinced that speaking in tongues was still alive and well in believers who asked for it.

A member of the Bible Study, Yvonne, told me in 1995 that she was going to a revival outside of Raleigh and invited me to come along. She knew that I wanted the gift of tongues and told me to pray about it as the revival would be a great place to receive it. I prayed about it and decided to go with her to the revival.

When we got there I was awestruck by how many people were there. It was a small church that probably had pew seating for 100+ worshippers. We got there about 15 minutes early and when we walked in I was amazed to find all the seats were full. Yvonne shouted and waved at someone in the altar area and they motioned her up. She went, hugged them, pointed to me, and motioned for me to come up to the front. I didn't understand why but I went anyway. As I walked by every pew I noticed that I was the only Caucasian there. Yvonne then pointed to the second pew in front of the pulpit and there was an empty spot there. She said they had saved that spot for me. Needless to say I was taken back. My spirit confirmed to me right then and there that this was going to be a very special service.

The Caucasian Christian community could learn a lot from our African American brothers and sisters. They really know how to worship. They not only sang with their mouths, but they sang with their whole bodies. They were jumping up and down, waving their arms in adoration of the Lord, and had smiles that went from ear to ear.

Soon it was time for the sermon. The guest preacher for the revival was Brother Mosley. When he started preaching the whole place erupted with praises of the Lord. I remember the feeling of the Spirit was so strong that it nearly knocked me over. When he got to the end of the sermon he offered the invitation.

Surprisingly no one came forward. I didn't understand as I was told that at African American revivals, just about everyone goes up during the invitation. He had them play the invitation song again and said, "Someone out there is waiting for a blessing and is going to miss it if they don't respond to God's invitation." I thought to myself, 'Is he talking about me?' I was afraid to go up in front of all these people I didn't know so I stayed in my pew.

When we finished the verse he had them play it again, one more time. He said again, "God is patient but the person that came here specifically to receive a blessing is going to miss their opportunity if they don't respond to God's call now."

Then I felt a spiritual nudge to go forward. Afraid, I moved out of the pew and walked up to the altar with my head down. Brother Mosley said to me, "Son. Why are you here?" I told him, "I am the one who is waiting for the blessing." He immediately said, "I know". I looked up just in time to see him reach up and touch my forehead. I immediately felt a sudden surge of energy into my body and I fell out, falling to the floor, speaking in tongues. When I awoke a few seconds later I felt someone's hands cradling my head while affirming that I had fallen out. Also my arms were raised up and I was praising God speaking in tongues. It was an indescribable feeling to feel God's love and Spirit so strongly. When I got my bearings I stood up and was going to go back to my pew. Brother Mosley told me to go the back of the altar and stand with the rest of the folks that he had subsequently touched and had been slain in the Spirit. I did so not knowing what was going to happen next.

Brother Mosley then proceeded to walk among the pews, touching people on their foreheads causing them to fall out all over the church. There was an unbelievable power in the sanctuary from the Holy Spirit moving among the people.

When he had finished moving among the pews Brother Mosley came back to the altar, walked by each of us and affirmed to us God's love.

When he came to me he reached out, touched me, and I was slain in the Spirit again, falling out and speaking in tongues.

The service ended soon thereafter and I went over to rejoin Yvonne and the others in our group. As I was making my way to the front door, Brother Mosley came by, looked at me, smiled and before I knew it, had touched me and I fell out a third time, I fell to the floor, speaking in tongues again. When I rose up Yvonne said I had a smile on my face that only God could give. All the way home I couldn't stop talking about how I was blessed with God answering my prayer and giving me the gift of tongues.

In May of 1996 I attended the Local Pastor's School for 2 weeks and loved every minute of it. There were about 15 of us, all eager to get into ministry. We had classes every day on the 'nuts and bolts' of being a pastor. We learned things like how to be the administrator of the church including how to correctly fill out all the District and Conference forms; how to conduct marriages, funerals and baptisms; how to prepare a sermon; a short course on Methodist History; and how to preach. We all became very close and kept in touch after we graduated. Usually we met each year at Annual Conference at Lake Junaluska, North Carolina. I felt really good being there and felt in my soul that God wanted this. Since I had male roommates I couldn't crossdress during the whole 2 weeks but I didn't really miss it that much as I was so immersed into learning.

Half of the graduates of the Local Pastor's School had appointments waiting for them when they finished. The other half, including me, did not. We had to wait, hope, and pray. A year later, May of 1997, I got a call from the District Superintendant that would result in my first appointment as a local pastor in the United Methodist Church.

The District Superintendent said he got a call from Lander's Chapel in Lincolnton, a church that I had preached at as a lay speaker. They liked me and wanted me to be their part-time pastor. I was thrilled! I said yes and started in July of 1997. Also in July of 1997 I started a part-time job as Curator of Life Sciences at the Schiele Museum of Natural History in Gastonia, North Carolina. Now with both part-time jobs and Pam's job, we were able to make ends meet financially.

While there I did my first funeral (a retired professor in the Agriculture Department at North Carolina State University) that was attended by several hundred friends and relatives. I was scared to death as it was my first funeral but everything went well. During my 10 years there I performed a total of 25 funerals, 2 weddings, and 15 baptisms. There weren't a lot of kids there as it was an older congregation. We did have a youth group, around 12 at its peak, that put on programs for the local church every Christmas and these were always highly anticipated.

Lander's Chapel was founded in 1845 by Rev. Samuel Lander and during its 'hey day' the church was the center of that area of Lincolnton known as the Lander's Chapel community. It had a local one room schoolhouse. It was also the polling station and the place where everyone in the community got the low down on what was happening. Then the demographics changed. The local mill closed down and many people moved away, including members of the church. This left some older members to carry the load of keeping the church open.

When I came I wanted desperately to try to do something to bring back the glory days again. We reached out to the community again by occasionally providing meals to the local prison. We held community meals once a month including taking free meals to those in the community we knew were shut-in and needed assistance. We also took 10 angels every Christmas from the Salvation Army Angel Tree for 10 years. I was involved in teaching Bible study and counseling at one of the local drug rehab centers, Cornerstone Ministry. Other community activities that the church did included: volunteering to cook lunch, when scheduled, for the soup kitchen in Lincolnton; rotating every 4 years in hosting the community Thanksgiving and Easter Sunrise services; hosting a monthly area senior citizens group meeting along with activities; conducting a number of fund raisers including manning a hamburger/hotdog booth at the annual Apple Festival in Lincolnton; raising money to help pay for medical treatment for a community member who had leukemia; and fund raisers for the local Lander's Chapel School House renovations. But it just wasn't enough. Only a couple families joined who had kids and I knew they wouldn't stay if more families with kids didn't become members too. So I came up with a plan.

The church owned the Lander's Chapel Schoolhouse. It had been used a long time ago as a scouting center for the church and the choir practiced there. But it had not been used for over 10 years and was falling into disrepair. I saw a great opportunity to use the schoolhouse and also to revive the Lander's Chapel community pride again. I drew up a proposal: Since the schoolhouse was the only one-room schoolhouse in the area left that still had its original integrity (there were originally three—one was gone and the other one had been converted into a home and had lost its original integrity), we could apply to Duke Endowment for a grant to restore the exterior as a schoolhouse and renovate the interior into a community center, providing space for programs to draw young families. Many of the families in the church supported the proposal. They even put together an internal committee to direct the proposal.

Early in my ministry at Lander's Chapel, I looked into going to Gordon-Conwell Theological Seminary in Charlotte and the Methodist Church agreed to recommend me. I got in, started taking classes in 1997 and took classes for a year. I met a number of seminary students in my classes and made some new friends. Part of the reason for going was, again, in hopes that while in one of the classes God would miraculously come to me and tell me why I was feeling like I was. But that never happened. Even though I loved learning about the scripture, I felt awkward. I was always afraid that I would somehow, inadvertently, say or do something that would give me away. I hated always being afraid. I wanted so desperately to just be able to be me.

I stopped going to Gordon-Conwell after about a year as the Methodist Church stopped accrediting their program for ordination. I applied to a special program (Course of Study) through the United Methodist Church at Duke Seminary for pastors who can't financially go to seminary full time. It required you to attend the month of July for 5 years. After completing the program you would get an M. Div. equivalent certificate. I started in 1998, completing the program in

2002 and received my Certificate. I loved going to Duke and did very well, graduating with a very high grade point average.

While at Duke I cross dressed every chance I could. I had a roommate and whenever he was gone I would cross dress. I never got caught (I was getting good at not getting caught). But my heart was getting heavier and heavier. I felt I was living a lie. I was presenting myself to the world as this good, wholesome, man with high values and inside I was longing to be a woman, dying a little every day. In my search for an answer at seminary, in all my prayers, I never felt the Holy Spirit tell me why I longed to be a woman. I had hoped that I would get an answer by drawing close to God in scripture and prayer. But alas, I felt more and more trapped. The harder I tried to quit, the more I needed it.

As is the United Methodist system, pastors get moved periodically so that churches can get new ideas and energy from a different pastor. I stayed there at my first appointment at Lander's Chapel United Methodist Church for 10 years. I loved the people very much.

But some influential members of the church didn't like the idea of renovating the old schoolhouse. They went to the District Superintendent and requested, behind everyone's back including mine, that the District move me. When the local church and I found out I was going to move we all were upset. I believe to this day that the main reason I was asked to be moved was because of my support of using the schoolhouse for a community center. These influential members wanted to tear the schoolhouse down and build a new fellowship hall instead and I was standing in their way. But unfortunately by this time it was too late for anyone to do anything to stop my move. It was approved and the District asked me to fill in at another church in Lincolnton, Rhyne Heights United Methodist, whose pastor was being treated in Winston-Salem for pancreatic cancer.

I stayed at Rhyne Heights for 6 months during the time their pastor was receiving treatments. I visited their pastor while he was in the hospital with some of the parishioners, reading the scripture to him and praying with him. Every Sunday I gathered the congregation together at the front of the church, asking everyone to form a circle and hold hands while we prayed for Pastor John. This simple gesture gave everyone a chance to reach out to each other in their common bond of love and fear for their pastor. We faithfully prayed for his healing and God answered our prayers. Pastor John received the ultimate healing through his death. Now he is totally healed and resting in peace with no more pain.

I was very blessed to see how God worked wonders in the ways that He healed them from the loss of their pastor who they loved very much. Pastor John taught them well as they strengthened each other and ultimately became a much stronger church as the result of his death. It was while at this church I agreed to do a fund raising event that ended up changing my life.

My first Christmas
December 1949

Me at Wilma Apartments
1950

Me with Grandma Reynolds
Fall 1951

Two volunteers doing therapy with
Davy on Patterning Table, c1974

Andy (9 months) and Davy
(4 ½ years) March, 1977

My hospital tag while clergy
with United Methodist church
1997-2007

Me and Pam at Braves Game
Atlanta 2000

Me and Pam in Charleston, SC
June 5, 2011

Me in my Relay For Life
Pageant gown, April 17, 2008

Me in part-time transition
July 2009

Glamour Shots, 2009
2 years before SRS
(Many say I look like Jamie Lee Curtis here)

Me in full-time transition
February 2010

With Donna in Trinidad, Colorado
October 5, 2010

My new breasts, August 6, 2010
(34 days after surgery)

SRS Hospital, Montreal, Canada,
taken January 19, 2011

Me and Felicia just before surgery
January 11, 2011

SRS Recovery Facility
Montreal, Canada taken
January 10, 2011

Me and Paige the day before leaving
Montreal, January 20, 2011

20 days after SRS, January 31, 2011
(photo taken by Lorrie Rankin)

Chapter 6
The Pageantry of it All

While at my firsy church appointment I volunteered at a drug rehab center doing Bible studies. The center was at a church that closed and the leaders of the center bought the buildings for a rehab center. The men each had rooms downstairs and shared a common TV room and bathroom. The men were required to attend worship every Sunday and AA and NA meetings each day. They could attend Sunday worship upstairs or, after their first month, attend any church in the community they desired. The program was very successful with close to a 50% success rate.

The men were not allowed to leave the main campus during their first month for any reason other than medical and then it had be under supervision. Their room and board was free during the first month, being paid through donations to the center. During the second month the men were helped by staff to find a job. They were encouraged to find jobs in fields that they were trained in or if they desired they could go into a new field. When they got a job, a small percentage of their pay check was garnished to help defray the cost of living at the center.

The center's program was so well respected in the community that there were a number of businesses that supported and welcomed the men. When they found work they were required to find their own transportation be it their own car or a ride with someone outside the center. By the third month, if the men had found work, they were assisted in finding a place to live. The plan was that if the men had a job and place to live, they could be released to live on their own by the end of the third month.

Frequently however it took longer to find work or a place to live so they stayed at the center longer. If they broke any rules, especially being caught with, or consuming any quantity of alcohol or drugs, they were expelled immediately from the program and not allowed to reapply for a year and only then with a referral letter from a physician.

I taught the men about God's forgiveness and hope, and treated them with respect. I loved being with the men and they greatly loved me. Each of them was very special to me. I never demeaned or condemned them for their addiction (i.e. 'you're going to hell if you don't repent and stop using drugs'). I continually told them that God loved them and wanted the best for them. I frequently ate meals with them at the center. Two of the clients even came to my first church, after completing their first month, were baptized and became members. Unfortunately about three months later they relapsed and had to drop out of the program.

While serving at my second church, the receptionist at the Center asked me to do her a favor. Her church had been asked to be a sponsoring church in the local community Relay for Life Fund Raiser. Relay for Life was well known in the community for the money it raised each year for cancer research and it was an honor to be asked to be a sponsoring church. Relay wanted each sponsoring church in 2007 to enter a man in their Womanless Beauty Pageant. She said she had asked all the men at her church and they all refused. She looked at me with a smile and said, "I think I know someone who will. You will won't you?" I sensed she knew my leanings toward womanhood when she asked. I had never been in public as a woman before but I felt compelled to say yes. I wanted to raise money for cancer research but I also was scared about the idea of being in public as a woman.

It was a double edged sword. I feared ridicule but I also longed so much to be a woman. Deep down I felt if I agreed to do the Pageant that it would change my life forever and it did.

We talked about the contest requirements. Relay for Life said they didn't want parodies of women from the sponsors. In other words, they didn't want men with hairy chests, hairy legs, beards, etc. They wanted the men to look as much like women as possible. The contestants were told they would stand on platforms and as people would come by, they would vote with money they put in a box near the platform. So the better you looked the more money you would raise. If I was going to participate I wanted to do the best I could and raise the most money possible for Relay for Life. She and a co-worker at the center agreed to help me learn how to act like a woman and to do my makeup. Now we had to decide what I would wear.

After some discussion, we decided I should be a bride since brides have a special beauty about them. It was exciting enough to be a woman in public, but to be a bride! It was almost too much. What girl doesn't dream of being a bride? In fact I had dreamed about being a bride for Halloween when growing up, along with being a princess, but could never tell Mom and Daddy. The co-worker brought her wedding dress into the Center for me to try on (she said she was about my size when she got married). She told me to find a pair of white heels and have them ready for when she brought in the dress. We decided I could safely try it on in the weight room when the men were having their Bible Study.

When the ladies recommended trying the dress on in the weight room I felt kind of strange. A weight room clearly has masculine symbolism. And here I was, a man who was definitely not very masculine going into a masculine weight room to put on a dress. They said it was the largest room in the building and had a big mirror so I reluctantly agreed.

I found a beautiful pair of white patent leather heels (about 3 ½") and put them in the car before my next visit to the Center. At the next visit they showed me the wedding dress. When I saw it and the veil I was so excited I almost cried. It was so beautiful! It was off-white with embroidery on the bodice and sleeves.

The lady who owned the dress told me to take it into the weight room, put it on, and call her on her cell phone and she would bring Keisha, the receptionist. As I walked to the weight room, I was afraid my heart was going to pound out of my chest. I was so excited I could hardly stand it. I found the mirror and a small area in front of it to put the dress on. I struggled getting my clothes off and putting the wedding dress on as it was pretty tight quarters. I unzipped the back and stepped into the dress. I pulled it up my body and slid my arms into the sleeves. I was afraid the sleeves may be too tight but amazingly the bride who wore the dress had the same size arms as mine. I grabbed the back of the dress and pulled it up toward my head so I could reach the zipper. After a while I finally got it, pulled it and was successful in zipping it up. I pulled the train around and since it was short there was room to spread it out in the weight room. I refrained from looking into the mirror until after I put the heels and veil on. Then I turned and looked in the mirror.

My heart was pounding while putting the dress on but when I looked in the mirror, I lost my breath. I couldn't believe how good I looked even without a bra, makeup and earrings. For the first time in my life I felt beautiful. I started fantasizing that I was getting ready for my wedding, getting ready to walk down the aisle to meet my future husband. This was the first time that I had ever thought about a relationship with a man. It was scary as I loved Pam so much but it all felt so natural as the dress made me feel like a bride.

When I was dressed, I called the co-worker who owned the wedding dress so she could get Keisha to surprise her. She came to the weight room and quietly knocked on the door. When I opened the door and she saw me she gasped. I asked her if she was okay and she smiled and said I looked beautiful. She fiddled with my dress and veil for a few minutes and after she was satisfied she told me to stand still as she was going to get Keisha.

Soon she came back with Keisha. When she opened the door and Keisha saw me, Keisha put her hand over her mouth, squealed, and jumped up and down. She also said I looked beautiful. I found myself smiling too as I loved the feelings I was having with the affirmation the two women gave me.

They both wanted me to go across the hall to show the two ladies that were working over there. I wasn't sure as I didn't want the men to see me. They assured me that the men wouldn't see me so I agreed. The two women there were also impressed. One of them couldn't believe how naturally I walked in 3 ½" heels. I couldn't believe it either but they felt good and I had no problem keeping my balance. It was like I had been walking in high heels all my life. After we talked for a couple minutes Keisha decided I needed to go back across the hall to the weight room and take the dress off. Reluctantly I agreed. I went back to the weight room and took the shoes, veil, and wedding dress off. As I did, I felt sad. I now understand why brides feel so beautiful on their wedding day. I felt it inside while wearing the wedding dress. I put my boy clothes back on and gave the wedding dress back to its owner.

To the best of my knowledge the men never saw me in the dress. I did not go out and show them or flaunt myself in front of them. The men saw me as an authority figure, a minister, a man of God, and I did not want to damage our relationship as they probably would not understand why I was in the Pageant.

The next time I went to the Center to teach a Bible Study with the men, Keisha and I got together to talk about the Pageant. We decided that even though I looked great in the wedding dress it would not lend itself well to walking outside in a football field. I agreed so we decided I should get a prom dress. It would be very pretty and be more manageable.

I was afraid to go into a dress shop and buy a prom dress dressed as a male. I also wasn't sure I could afford a prom dress as I knew they could be expensive. Keisha asked her pastor to write me a letter explaining that I needed the prom dress for a fund raising event and asked if they could donate the dress. I felt a little better but I didn't want to go alone so I asked a female friend, Deborah Baliles, if she would go with me to buy the bra and prom dress. She agreed and we went to the local mall. I took the white heels and a pair of clip-on hoop earrings.

We chose a day and hoped for the best. We went to a couple of stores to look for a bra. Either they were too expensive or the clerks gave us dirty looks when they read the pastor's letter. We finally found a strapless bra off the sale rack at Dillard's for a very good price (we decided on a strapless bra as we didn't know if the eventual prom dress required it. Either way we were fine). We then took the new bra, heels, and earrings and went to Bedazzled (prom and wedding dress shop) to look at prom dresses.

I told the clerk there that I needed a prom dress for a fund raising pageant and she was extremely helpful. She put me at ease quickly. In fact she treated me like she would have any teenage girl coming in to buy her prom dress. She took me back into the changing rooms and had me take my shirt and pants off. She had me put my bra on and stuff it with hose. She measured my bust (with the stuffed bra) and waist. She said I should get a separate top (large) and a size 10 skirt as my measurements did not fit a normal girl. I looked at the rack and found three that I liked. Two of them did not look good on but the third one was a winner. It was a very pretty blue with balls along the bottom of the top. The skirt was ¾ length so it covered my bony knees. When the clerk zipped the top up, she smiled and said I looked good. I then put the heels and earrings on.

When we left the dressing room she led me over to the mirrors (3 mirrors with two at angles so you could see your back) that were about 25 feet from the dressing rooms. As we walked over to the mirrors the clerk commented on how well I was walking in the 3 ½" heels saying she couldn't do that. On the way to the mirrors, one of the other clerks saw me, smiled, and said, "You look stunning". I almost cried right there. I continued walking to the mirrors and my jaw dropped when I saw myself. I looked amazing. Again I almost cried. My feelings were so overpowering. I really liked what I saw and it felt right. The clerk then proceeded to tell me what jewelry would go with the dress and I listened intently. We then walked back to the dressing room where I took the dress, bra, earrings, and heels off. I changed back into my 'boy clothes' which didn't feel right.

I then went to the counter to pay for the dress. I showed the cashier the letter from the pastor asking for the prom dress to be donated as the pageant was for charity. She said she would have to get the store manager. He came over and complimented me on using the dress for a charity function but said he was sorry but he could not donate the dress. He said he was donating a number of dresses to the local high schools for girls who couldn't afford prom dresses (the schools proms were coming up in a week). He did say he would sell it to me at a reduced price though (50% off). So I got a $300 dress for $150. The two clerks who helped me told me to be sure and come back after the pageant as they wanted to see pictures of me in the prom dress. I thanked them both and promised I would come back with pictures.

Then next day I took the prom dress to the Center to show Keisha and the co-worker who let me try on her wedding dress. I couldn't take it into the Center so I had the ladies come out to my car. They both were excited and couldn't wait to see me in it. Keisha said she had a beautiful necklace and earring set that would go perfectly with the dress. When she brought them the next time I came to teach I found out the earrings were for pierced ears. Keisha just assumed I had pierced ears. Now I wished I did as the earrings were beautiful.

The next day, while talking again with Keisha at the Center, I found out she wanted to organize a womanless beauty pageant there, at the Center, to help raise money for the Center. She wanted the guys to participate and she also asked me to participate. Of course I said yes as it was again a way to raise money for a good cause.

She said that there would also be a talent segment to the Center pageant. I told her I couldn't sing or play an instrument. Then she said, "But you could lip sync to a song from a CD". I thought about it and decided to lip sync to 'These Boots Are Made for Walkin'' by Nancy Sinatra. I could get a go-go dress and go-go boots and it would be fun. She agreed and thought that would be great. I decided to go out to the store and get a copy of Nancy Sinatra's greatest hits so I could practice lip-synching to the song. I went to Best Buy and found the CD I needed. I also found a karaoke CD with the 'Boots' song on it and bought that too.

I went online and ordered a paisley go-go dress with multiple colors and a lot of yellow in my size. It came within a couple weeks. When I got it I couldn't wait to try it on. It fit great and I was amazed again at how good women's clothes looked on me. Since the dress had a lot of yellow in it and the model pictured on the packaging insert had yellow go-go boots, I decided I needed to get yellow go-go boots too.

To minimize stares and chances of being beat up, I decided to go to a costume store in a nearby town dressed as a woman to see if they had any yellow go-go boots, carrying the go-go dress with me. I wore a white blouse, black skirt, and white heels. I did my hair, makeup and put on a pair of hoop clip-on earrings. I was ready to go. I got in the car, said a prayer, and was on my way.

When I got to the store I hesitated as to whether to go in. Even though I felt I looked good, I was still apprehensive that someone may see through me. I decided I had to chance it. I took a deep breath, got out of the car and went into the costume store. I went to the counter. I showed the clerk the go-go dress in the bag and told her I needed some yellow go-go boots to match the dress as I was in a pageant. She looked at me and smiled which put me at ease. She said she didn't think they had any yellow go-go boots to match the dress. She then went over and told an older lady (probably the head clerk) what I needed. This lady looked at me suspiciously but said they did not have any yellow go-go boots. I took a deep breath, said thank you and proceeded to leave. A young man, with his 8-10 year old son, was coming into the store as I was leaving the store. He held the door for me. I thanked him, and he smiled back, replying, "You're welcome ma'm". I got chills. It made me feel good. Clearly he didn't know. I totally passed. It felt so good to know I passed as this was my first time in public dressed as a woman (regardless that it was a costume store).

I drove home, changed out of the female clothes and decided to order the yellow go-go boots online. I went to eBay again and ordered them from a store in the states that got them from Korea. They came in a couple weeks and they looked great with the go-go dress. I was thrilled. I felt like I had a chance to raise a lot of money for the Center. I was getting more and more excited. I was ready to "go-go".

Unfortunately the Center Pageant never materialized. The Center Director said no to it as he felt it was demeaning to the men.

Yet I was continuing to get mixed feelings about the pageant. I was excited about the opportunity to present myself as the woman I felt I truly was but I was afraid of my friends leaving me when they found out or saw me. The pageant was for Relay for Life and almost everyone in town went to this fund raiser as cancer is no respecter of persons. We all know someone, a friend, family, or church member, who has battled the awful disease. I continued to practice presenting myself as a woman at home when Pam wasn't there. I got very comfortable in my 3 ½" high heels and learned to walk in them well.

As I was always looking for information on the internet on being transgendered, I stumbled on a website by a professional hypnotist in Illinois named Dawn Slavings. She offered a series of hypnotism CD's for sale that were designed to help transgendered women to feel more comfortable with themselves and therefore present themselves better as women. I thought – these CD's could help me present myself better at the pageant. So I ordered the first CD. After I listened to it, I felt myself filled with joy. I felt the joy of being a woman deep within myself. I was excited now more than ever. With the help of the hypnotism CD, I was able to be more relaxed, present myself better and raise more money than ever for Relay for Life. And as an added bonus, I would feel better about myself.

One night, a couple of weeks before the pageant, I decided to dress up and present myself to Pam. I wanted so much for her to feel comfortable about it but I feared the worst. I remembered some of her earlier comments about some of my feminine looks (long hair, long nails, hair scunci's, and ponytail) and was afraid. But I felt I needed to be out front and do it. I took a couple hours and did it all – underwear, prom dress, makeup, jewelry, heels. I sat in the chair by the TV and waited for her to come home. I would know when she drove up the driveway as Murphy, our cat, would let me know. When she drove up, Murphy hollered. I took a deep breath and stood up. When she opened the door and saw me she gave me a disgusted look. I feared the worst. She asked me why I was dressed like a girl. I told her I was asked to be in a Womanless Beauty Pageant for Relay for Life and I was practicing. Then she came over and started primping me. She messed with my hair and tugged on my dress. She looked at me and for the first time in the journey, smiled. My fear and apprehension went away. She said that if I was going to win this pageant I needed some help.

She told me to take off the clothes and she would take me shopping. She said my hair was too thin and I needed a hair piece. I went to the bathroom, took off the clothes (unhappily because they felt normal), put on 'boy' clothes and we went to two beauty supply stores in town. The first one did not have any hair pieces but we finally were able to find one at Sally's Beauty Shop in town.

When we went in we were honest with the clerk. We told her we were looking for a hair piece for me as I was in a fund raising pageant for Relay for Life. She gave her support and was very willing to help us find a small hair piece that had a comb in it and its color matched my natural color well. Pam also picked up some pretty hair pins to put in the hair piece. As we left the clerk asked me to bring her a picture after I got all dressed for the pageant. I smiled and told her I would be happy to return with a pageant picture.

I still don't know what caused Pam to all of a sudden be supportive. Whether she finally came to accept it when she saw me dressed or she truly wanted me to do well. Either way, I really don't care. I just knew I was happy that she was helping me be the best I could be.

Finally the big day came – April 17, 2008. I worked at the Museum during the day and went to my hairdresser to get my hair done for the pageant. As I drove to the hairdressers I worried about someone seeing through me as her shop was next to a busy psychiatrist. When I pulled up I was hoping I would be coming during a lull in the psychiatrist's client visits, but I was not that lucky. There were so many that they were lined up outside. I just took a deep breath and went to the door. I was pleased that no one noticed me.

When I got into the hairdressers I sat down to wait for my appointment. The lady sitting next to me started talking to me and I responded in my highest female voice. She was nice and didn't seem to know or care. Olivia's daughter, Jade, walked by me and gave me a concerned look. She then went back to her mom and I heard her say, "Is something wrong with Duane? He's out there dressed as a girl." Olivia proceeded to tell her that I was in a pageant raising money for Relay for Life. Jade then came out and complimented me on my bravery to do that. The lady next to me also complimented me and said I made a very nice looking woman. Olivia finally called me back and did my hair.

She did an 'up-do' with tight curls. She said it would look the best as my hair was a little thin. She also said it should hold through the pageant. She lied. By the time I got home it had already started to fall and by the time Pam got home it had almost totally fallen. I was upset and Pam was fit to be tied. She couldn't believe the hairdresser couldn't do better than that. Pam then took me back to the bedroom vanity and worked for a half hour to fix my hair. When she finished it looked great.

I did my makeup but didn't put the dress on. It had rained the previous night and I didn't want the dress to get muddy going across a wet football infield. We agreed I should put the dress on when I got there. We sat at the dining room table and Pam did my nails in a pretty mauve color. As she did my nails Pam gave me hints on how to carry myself and what not to do. When we were ready we got into the car and Pam drove to the football field. When we got there I told Pam, "I don't know whether I can do this." Pam quickly said, "It's too late to back down now". I took a deep breath and got out of the car.

On the way to the infield I called Keisha's cell phone and she met me and Pam with a number of members of her church. They all cheered when they saw me and said I looked beautiful even without the gown. I asked where I could change assuming they had a tent. Keisha said things got messed up and they didn't have a tent. One of the ladies from her church told me where the ladies rest room was and said I could change there. I said I better not as I didn't want to start a commotion. All the members of Keisha's church said no one would know. I still didn't want to go there to change. Pam and I eventually found members of our previous church who had raised a tent on the infield. They recognized me and told me I could change there. They cleared it out and Pam and I went in to change. I had trouble getting the top on with the falsies and padding that I had in the bra. Pam told me to take the padding out. I did and the top finally fit. I put the 3 ½" white heels on and walked out of the tent. When I exited two members of our church smiled and took my picture.

I found Keisha and she said that the rules for the pageant had been changed at the last minute. Anyone could participate including parodies of women (men with hairy chests and legs, balloon boobs, etc.) which would explain why I saw them coming onto the playing field. Also, now, the contestants had one hour to go all over the infield and beg for donations. Most of the contestants had come early so they had been getting donations for the last hour. I didn't bring a purse so I had to borrow a large tote bag. I walked for what seemed 'a mile', begging for donations and battling my heels as they sank deep into the wet infield. I told everyone I was a poor girl that needed help for the pageant and they bought it. Most said they had already given money to previous contestants but gave me a few dollars anyway. I only had 45 minutes and was able to raise $300 which I thought was good.

When it came time for the pageant to start (around 11pm), they asked the pageant contestants to come to the top of the bleachers on one side of the ball field to be interviewed. They asked us to walk across the front of the bleachers and go up the stairs to the top of the bleachers where the radio booths were so we could parade in front of the Relay crowd. It felt good to walk across the front of the bleachers in front of everyone until I had to go up the stairs. When I changed into the two piece dress, Pam gave me a half-slip to put under the skirt so it would lie better. We didn't know that I would have to climb a bunch of stairs. The slip made it very hard to raise my legs high enough to go up the stairs but I made it and didn't fall once.

They told us when we got to the back of the radio booth to give them our money. It was very muddy back there and all of us in heels were having trouble not falling. I gathered my money from my tote bag and handed it to them. Then they handed us a short questionnaire to fill out. It was basic questions that they would use when they interviewed us. At the top of the questionnaire they asked us our female name. I hadn't really thought of it before. I put the pen on the line and immediately wrote Dawn. It was natural. Everyone else wrote down a catchy name like 'Blues Baby'. But I wrote Dawn because I knew in my heart that was who I had always been. It signified the dawn of a new beginning, a new life. A perfect fit.

They lined us up along the back wall behind the radio booth. As we filed into the bleachers they took our names and told us to stand in a line up against the back wall facing out to the audience which was gathered on the infield in front of us. Then the two moderators went down the line, calling each contestant out to interview them. The two moderators were positioned on both ends of the line. As they went down the line and came closer to me I started to formulate in my mind what I was going to say. When they finished the contestant in front of me they called the name of the contestant behind me. They skipped me. I became agitated. After they finished with the last contestant I told the moderator closest to me they had skipped me. They checked their list and acknowledged they had accidently missed me. One of the moderators called my name, Dawn, and he interviewed me, telling the audience I had been accidently skipped. He asked me if I wasn't too old for the pageant. I told him, "I cannot tell a lie. I just turned 16". Everyone in the audience laughed. Afterwards Pam said I had the best interview. Then they announced the winner. The winner was determined by the amount of money they raised, NOT by how good they looked. The winning contestant won with over $600 (I think he had checks from friends and had raised the money before the pageant started). He was a young kid, probably not over 16 years of age, had a baby face and did make a good looking girl. Pam told me later that he was probably the best looking girl in the bunch (there were 15 contestants) but she said I had the best presentation. Even though I didn't win, I still was proud of what I had done.

I walked the track afterwards (around midnight) during the Memory Walk (lighted bags with names of loved ones who died of cancer lined the inside and outside of the track). It was a very moving walk. Pam paid a donation to have a bag put out with my mom's name as she died of brain cancer in March, 1984. During the walk a couple of high school boys came by me and said, "Please tell me you're a girl". I told him, "I'm sorry. I wish I was but I'm not a girl". They said I had to be a girl. I smiled as their comment made me feel good.

Before the night was over, Pam took some pictures of me on the track. The pictures turned out well but they really didn't show the joy in my eyes. We finally got home around 2am and I was very tired. It had been a great event, raising thousands of dollars for cancer research and I think the audience enjoyed the pageant. After the pageant I found myself going back to look at my picture and remembering how good it made me feel. Even though I was scared, it still felt right and I was glad I did it. I also knew in my heart that my life would never be the same again.

Chapter 7
Rejected Ministry

After the pageant I struggled with wanting to be a woman all the time. It just made me feel so good inside when I was dressed as a woman. In the succeeding four visits to my hairdresser I went dressed as Dawn. My hair style was a unisex style so the way I was dressed had no bearing on the clothes I wore. Olivia smiled each time I went and didn't hesitate to cut my hair. Once, when she called me Duane, I asked her to call me Dawn as it felt wrong to call me by a male name when I was dressed as a woman. She didn't do it, but seemed to go along with everything. Each time I left the salon, I went home, took the female clothes off, and reluctantly put my boy clothes back on. The journey to get my hair cut became an activity that I looked forward to as it gave me some time to relax and relieve all the internal stress I was dealing with.

A pivotal event in my life occurred in January 2008. Daddy died of congestive heart failure at the age of 83. He had lived a full life and was ready to die. His relationship with Jesus was so good that I marvel everyday at how much peace he felt when he died and how he went with no struggle. Like with Mom, I never told Daddy that I had gender identity issues because I didn't want to hurt him. I held his hand a few hours before he died. At that very special moment he told me, "Son. Know that I love you, I have always been proud of you and nothing you could ever do or say will change that."

Did Daddy know and wasn't telling me out of love and respect for me? Today I want to think he did as believing that makes me feel better inside knowing that Daddy loved me regardless. Nothing in our relationship would make me feel otherwise. Daddy did everything with me when I grew up and was the best example and model for me that a son could have. It wasn't his fault that I had the gender identity issues. He did everything right. It was me. Even with the best model and example, internally I couldn't feel good about being a man. With both Mom and Daddy gone I was now free to be the woman I really was.

The Pageant had already changed my life. Up until that time I had feared that if I expressed my true self, the woman who I felt I was, I would immediately be detected as a man and be ridiculed and scorned. But that wasn't the case at the Pageant. I was accepted, admired, and even told I couldn't be a man under the dress. It opened my eyes. I could be my true self if I was careful and did it in a safe environment. I wanted so desperately to be free to express the female in me that I searched for ways I could without being detected.

Over the last three years as a Methodist pastor I had let my hair grow. It now was long and I pulled it back in a pony tail. This was irregular for a Methodist pastor. In fact, I believe I was the only Methodist pastor in the District who had a pony tail (the District had over 90 churches). No one in the church (local, District, or Conference) asked me to cut it even though there were some in all three levels that told me I looked better with short hair. I liked keeping it long as it gave me opportunities to do it up in a female style (set it with rollers, make a flip) when I was alone. I looked in the mirror after I had done my hair up, applied makeup and earrings, and I saw the woman I truly was. I never saw a man trying to look like a woman. I hated it when I had to take off the makeup and straighten my hair. It made me sad. Each time I did it I became more content in 'female mode' and less content in 'male mode'.

The other thing I started doing was filing and shaping my fingernails. After filing and shaping them I would paint them with clear fingernail polish. Quite a few members of my last church appointment looked with scorn on me and questioned why I wanted fingernails that looked like a woman's. I would always tell them, "I'm growing them long so I can use them as forceps when handling small bugs (as I was a part-time entomologist) and the polish was to keep them from breaking." My statement was true but growing my fingernails long also made me feel good emotionally. Most of my parishioners accepted my explanation but many were skeptical.

When I dressed in the privacy of my home when Pam was gone, I would paint them with red and pink nail polish. I loved the way they looked. Most of the time I couldn't leave the polish on long because I had to give myself time to remove it and air out the fingernail polish remover smell from the bathroom before Pam got home. Just being able to keep it on for 5 minutes was a great joy.

The church that I was currently serving, Rhyne Heights United Methodist in Lincolnton, was still recovering from the death of their beloved pastor. Since Pastor John died in the middle of the appointment year, the Conference decided to leave me to assist them in their healing until the new appointments were made in the spring.

The pageant was during this healing period so I never mentioned it to the church. I did it unknown to anyone. I felt I was not under any obligation to tell them as the pageant was for charity and I was sure they wouldn't mind anyway.

When the new appointments came out in the spring the Methodist church moved me to another struggling church, Trinity United Methodist, in my hometown of Gastonia. The church leaders at Rhyne Heights fought for me to stay there but the Bishop said since I was only part-time I had to move as Rhyne Heights needed a full time pastor.

At Trinity I became embroiled in a number of problems that occurred during the previous pastor's appointment. But the church was responsive to me and I felt that I was doing well in helping the healing. Pam even came, joined, and took part in the chancel choir. It was the first time Pam attended the church I served as she didn't want to be scrutinized as the pastor's wife. It seemed all was going well. At least it felt like it on the outside even as I was still struggling on the inside.

After I went through the divorce with Shirley and was stressed so much that I planned suicide, I promised myself then that I would NEVER go through another divorce. Therefore I told myself I had to do whatever it took to save my marriage with Pam even if that meant that I had to fulfill my female longings 'in the closet'.

Not long after I started serving at this new appointment, my District Superintendant, Rev. Patricia Lewis, called me. She said she needed to meet with me as there were some serious accusations being brought against me. I said I would be there the next day. When I met with her she told me I was being accused of being a habitual cross dresser. She had reports that I was seen all over Gastonia dressed as a woman. I told her that was not true. The only times I was in public dressed as a woman was associated with the pageant which she knew about. I told her that I went to the hairdresser 4 times dressed as a woman to prepare for the pageant and had gone to the costume store, Morrison's Costumes in Charlotte, to get some go-go boots for another pageant (which never materialized but I didn't tell her that). But each time I returned from an outing, I told her that I immediately took the female clothes off. She then told me some shocking statements.

She said that she had received a call from a member of the church I was serving. The member said that when I had told her about the pageant from last year that 'I was too comfortable with it'. She said I didn't tell her like most men would, being "fidgety" and uncomfortable with it. I told her with a glint in my eye, clearly enjoying doing it. She felt my response was inappropriate.

Rev. Lewis also said she had received a call from my hairdresser, Olivia, stating that I had been regularly going to have my hair cut dressed as a woman and wanted her to call me Dawn. I admitted to Rev. Lewis that, yes, I had done that (I didn't understand why my hairdresser had to tell my boss about that as I wasn't hurting anyone). Rev. Lewis said a hearing with the District Board of Ordained Ministry would be called to address the allegations. She told me it could cost me my job. I was very hurt by my hairdresser calling her and felt betrayed. I was afraid, as a result of her phone call to my District Superintendant, I might have to leave town.

When I left the District Superintendant's office I felt crushed. I clearly had been betrayed. Yes, when I had gone back to the hairdresser I had dressed as Dawn. Olivia didn't say anything negative each time so I didn't know that it bothered her. It just made me feel good inside to go as Dawn. Now my job and life in my hometown were in danger.

I knew the accusations that I had been shopping in town, as a woman, were false. Someone lied. Then I remembered an incident while serving at Rhyne Heights.

I longed so much to be a woman that I started putting makeup and earrings on and driving around town. I never left the car. I just wanted to be 'out' as a woman. That could account for the reports that I had been seen all over town. During one of my trips to go and see Davy (he was in a special Center that was taking care of him), I put lipstick and earrings on. I wore them while driving on I-40 to see Davy. I took them off when I got into town before getting to where Davy was staying. The Sunday after visiting Davy, a choir member mentioned to me that he had seen me on I-40 when I went to see Davy. He said he honked but I didn't respond (I was probably too intent on thinking about something to hear him). He apparently recognized my car and saw me in lipstick and earrings and told the District Superintendant. So from the outside it looked like I was a woman all the time.

Rev. Lewis called the chair of the Trinity's PPR (Pastor-Parish Relations) Committee which is the local church committee that I, the pastor, answer to. She told him about the accusations and said she wanted him to address them in a PPR Committee meeting as soon as possible. He called a PPR Committee meeting within a couple days.

In the meeting I didn't deny anything except that I was living as a woman on the side. I told them the same thing I told the District Superintendent. Most of the committee members were stunned by the accusations as I would have expected. The chairman said he was not going to judge me and would wait for more evidence. He said the truth would eventually come out. I definitely was scared, not knowing what was going to happen to me and my ability to effectively serve as a pastor in the United Methodist Church.

I also had been driving to work with lipstick and earrings on. It was a short distance (6 miles) from home to work so I didn't think anyone would see me. When I arrived at work, I would take the lipstick and earrings off before entering the building. I didn't consider that some of my parishioners might recognize my car and report it to the District Superintendant. Going out with lipstick and earrings on while driving seemed to be such an innocent thing and I didn't think it would cause a problem. Clearly many people saw me and got the wrong impression. Looking back I wish I had not done it but I probably would have eventually gotten caught anyway.

Even though only the PPR Committee members and the three who told the District Superintendent about the pageant knew what was going on, my effectiveness as a minister was definitely compromised. The feeling I was living a lie was increasing daily. Whenever I looked at anyone I felt condemnation even though they probably knew nothing about what was going on. I wasn't comfortable anymore as a pastor. It became clear to me that I had to resign from my appointment. I resigned from my last church, Trinity United Methodist on Sunday, July 27, 2008.

I went to see Rev. Lewis and told her I was going to resign. I asked her how I should do it. She suggested telling the congregation the following Sunday. As she knew that it would have been very difficult for me to tell them, she volunteered to tell them. I thanked her and took her up on her offer. She gave me permission to lead the worship that Sunday and I would invite her to come to the microphone during the sermon time and she would tell them then.

The service that Sunday was the hardest I ever led. I was clearly nervous and I think congregation could sense it. I had to stop a number of times to get control of my emotions. When it came time for the sermon I invited Rev. Lewis to come forward. I didn't know what she was going to say and really didn't worry about it as there was nothing I could do about it by that time. Then when she told them I was in total shock. She said I was resigning my appointment effective immediately due to personal reasons. She gave no details. She just said it was for personal reasons, which was true. I was very grateful she didn't elaborate. When I greeted everyone as they left I felt a deep loss. I loved the members and I profoundly felt I had let them down. It was one of the lowest times of my life. When I went home I cried for a long time and was drained.

I knew I had to eventually meet with the District Committee of Ordained Ministry (DCOM). I dreaded it for I knew it would be ugly. They were the Methodist Church's arm that approved my appointment to Trinity United Methodist and were ultimately responsible for my misconduct. The District Superintendent called me and said she had set the meeting for September 2, 2008.

I put my best suit on and tried to be positive. When I walked into the District office I took a deep breath and prayed for strength. I didn't have to wait long as the District Superintendent came out of the meeting room very soon after I got there and called me in. When I entered and saw the faces of the approximate 12 members present, of which most were ministers, I became petrified. I knew it was going to be difficult and my feelings were right on target. The chairman, Rev. Jim Westmoreland, asked me, as he did before each DCOM meeting, "What is going on?" I proceeded to tell him, and the committee, everything. I was totally honest and forthright with all that I knew and didn't hide anything. I figured they knew it all anyway and if I tried to hide it they would be even harder on me. During the whole meeting I was visibly shaking so the committee members had to know how difficult the meeting was for me. It all seemed so ironic. I had an excellent record as a pastor, was well loved by all but a few members of all the churches I had served. But now I was on the hot seat and accused of something I really wasn't guilty of. Yes, I was a habitual cross dresser but I was not parading myself all around town as I was being accused and I was still a good pastor. To my horror, every member of the committee, including the chairman and District Superintendant, dumped on me.

Most of the members started talking about either their personal experiences of pageants whether it was males dressing as women or of others whom they knew that participated in pageants. They all stressed strongly that in each situation that it was always in jest, fun, and those participating were parodies of women. I tried to explain that the contest rules didn't want parodies of women therefore I had to shave my legs and chest and look as much like a woman as possible so I could raise as much money as I could for the charity. No one listened. Everything I said in my defense was ignored. No one heard a word. And to add insult to injury, no one said anything supportive of me or my service record.

Everyone in the committee made fun of me and the whole situation, making statements that implied that my actions, including involvement with the Pageant, were totally inappropriate. At the end they implied I was sick by telling me that I needed professional help. They wanted me to see the Methodist Counselor. It was implied in most of their statements that my actions were not only inappropriate for a Methodist pastor but they were also inappropriate to God, inferring that God didn't approve of me as a pastor.

I left the meeting fighting back tears. I told the District Superintendant's secretary, "It is over. I won't be back". Within a couple days I received a letter from the District Superintendant stating that they recognized my spiritual gifts but they all said that I am seriously sick. The DCOM concurred that I needed to see the Methodist counselor in town within 3 months for an evaluation. After they received his report the DCOM would meet again and "determine if I was fit to remain a minister of the United Methodist Church and if I didn't go to see the counselor within the allotted time they would ask me to surrender my credentials".

After the meeting I wrote my hairdresser a letter expressing my discontent with the result of her phone call. It read:

Dear Olivia,

I just met with my District Board of Ordained Ministry (they are the board that recommends appointments to the Bishop and whether anyone retains their credentials in ministry).

The purpose of the meeting was to discuss the situation that forced me to resign my church appointment. The situation centered on my involvement with the Relay for Life womanless beauty pageant in 2007. You were so kind to fix my hair for the pageant for which I am very grateful.

However, as you know, I have come back for subsequent hair trims sometimes dressed as a woman. It was a way to relax and no harm was meant. I thought that was our secret. But apparently not, as my District Superintendent, revealed in our meeting this morning of her conversation with you about my subsequent visits. She even said I asked you to call me by a feminine name (I did ask you once I recall but you refused).

I am in serious trouble now. I will probably lose my credentials as a pastor and not be able to do any ministry in town again. Could you not have told her everything? Or said the subsequent visits were connected with the other pageant I was asked to be a part of (through the rehab Center)?

I am deeply hurt. I hope I will not have to move from town because of this, but I may. I am disappointed that you revealed so much information to her. *I'm sorry but I cannot come back to you feeling comfortable telling you anything. You broke my confidence in you.*

Best wishes in all your future business endeavors.

Duane Flynn

When I went to work on the next scheduled work day, I told my trusted co-worker, Carrie, that I needed to talk with her and asked her if she would go walk with me on the Museum Nature Trail. She said absolutely and I told her everything. I told her of all my fears. I cried periodically as I was terrified of my future. Like I had hoped she would, she supported me by telling me that I was not an evil person because I was trying to be myself. She said the church should have been the place where I should have found love but instead I found condemnation. She told me "whether you come to work in a dress or pants, you are still the same loving and caring person." Thank God for good friends.

When I went home I prayed about what had happened trying to find peace but instead I spiraled into depression. My feelings of being a failure were so strong. I started thinking again about suicide. I didn't want to go on living. On top of it all, Pam was really having a hard time with everything. Her issues were more with the church than my cross dressing. She reminded me of what she had told me before I entered the ministry. She said "church people can be some of the meanest people in the world." I told her she was overreacting when she said that but now I understand exactly what she meant. She didn't understand why I was having gender identity issues but she was very angry with the way the Methodist Church treated me. She thought they were being very insensitive to my feelings.

I kept praying about what to do. After much thought and prayer I came to realize three things: (1) that if I went to the Methodist Counselor as the DCOM recommended, he would probably not be unbiased in his evaluation and support the DCOM's position that I was sick and (2) even if, by some miracle after the counselor's report was sent to the DCOM and they decided to allow me to stay in the church as a pastor, I would probably have to go through many rounds of therapy that would make me feel worse about myself; and (3) that my record would be forever stained with this incident making it impossible for me to ever get a good appointment again. So after a month of prayer and reflection of my life, I decided I had to surrender my credentials. I saw no other option that I could live with. My life as a Methodist minister was over.

I wrote the following letter, September 15, 2008, to the Rev. Patricia Lewis, the Gastonia District Superintendant, enclosing my credentials:

Dear Rev. Lewis,

It is with deep hurt, great sadness, and a broken spirit that I voluntarily surrender my local pastor's license in the United Methodist Church.

After much prayer and internal retrospection, I have determined that the events and charges of improprieties that have been brought against me have compromised my effectiveness as a local pastor within the United Methodist church so extensively that it is not practical for me to continue.

I have admitted that during the events surrounding the two fundraising pageants for Relay for Life and local Rehab Center (during 2007). I made some bad choices and have done some things, that, in retrospect, I should not have done. But they were made, as I confessed, with the intent of doing the best job possible to raise the most money for the charities involved. In your September 4th follow-up letter from the DCOM meeting, it was mentioned that there were concerns about 'my propensity toward what may be 'obsessive-compulsive behavior'. I assume that was due to the choices I made that are in question. If we are honest with ourselves, we ALL have 'obsessive-compulsive' behavior tendencies toward things we have passions about. My so-called 'obsessive-compulsive' behavior was because of my passion for both causes.

Except for 6-10 individuals that I am aware of, the rest of the parishioners of the three churches that I had the privilege to serve, and my true friends, still believe in me. They know and love me for the compassionate man who gave unselfishly all he had for them. They know that I loved them and will always love them. I however, do not feel the DCOM recognizes me in that same way. Even though you said in the afore mentioned DCOM follow-up letter that the DCOM recognizes the effective way I have served the church in the past, I did not feel that at the called DCOM meeting regarding my situation. Granted, I was angry when I came in and was defensive in my remarks. But surely the Committee saw that I was hurting and scared. I did not feel any of the love and compassion that the Committee had shown me over the last 11 years I have been under their care. All I felt was chastisement and judgment. I felt like it was a 'witch-hunt'. That it was a basic formality and the Committee was there to just get 'more information', at my expense, to justify the decision that they felt was inevitable. I felt no spirit of reconciliation or forgiveness. No one, even those of the DCOM that have known me and knew of my ministry over the years, came to my defense. No one said anything in support of my ministry or character at all.

I am very disappointed in the Methodist Church. The current Methodist slogan being told in the media is 'Open doors, open minds, open hearts'. I felt none of that philosophy of faith during this process. Clearly, you, personally, have lost respect for me for I can see it in your eyes and attitude and the DCOM's as well. By the DCOM's attitude at the called Tuesday, September 2nd meeting, it was clear that they too, have lost their respect for me. Because of these existing attitudes, I have lost my trust in any official in the United Methodist Church. I have nothing personally against the DCOM's counseling recommendation of Dr. Arey, but I do not feel I could be open and talk about my feelings to any United Methodist counselor. I admit I need someone to talk to about feelings I have but I will continue to search outside the United Methodist church for that person. I thank God for my wife Pam, and true friends, whose love and compassion for me has given me hope to not give up on myself.

Because I'm too well known in the District and because of the situation in question, I cannot continue to worship in the United Methodist tradition. I cannot help but feel every clergyperson and leader within the District will be 'looking at me with disdain.' My ministry within the United Methodist Church is effectively over. For that reason, I will be leaving the United Methodist Church and seeking a place of worship where I can have a new start.

These experiences have put a bad taste in my mouth about parish ministry and the way the 'church' treats their own. I was for-

warned about how cruel ministry can be but I was blinded by my belief in the system.

I am not the evil person that I have been portrayed as. I love the Lord. I have served faithfully over the years that I have been appointed in the United Methodist Church. The Lord knows that and I know in my heart that He has forgiven me of anything that I may have said or done that was wrong even if the 'church' has not.

I must bring closure to these events and move on with my life. I will be praying for the Lord to open my eyes to the other forms of ministry He has planned for me. And I will be praying for the United Methodist Church. I will be praying that's God's forgiving spirit of compassion, forgiveness, and reconciliation will be restored.

Duane Flynn

During the whole time I was a minister in the United Methodist Church I never felt I was being untrue to my ministry calling. I knew in my heart God had called me into the ministry and I believe my fruit while a minister supports the calling. Never during my ministry did I feel that my gender identity disorder conflicted with my calling. Male or female, it doesn't matter. God calls the person not the gender. I never talked to anyone about my gender identity disorder therefore I was not in any way, shape, or form, proselytizing. I didn't understand the full meaning of my condition until much later and I certainly didn't want anyone to know about it. My gender identity disorder did not affect the way I felt about people as I loved all people as God loves them with no prejudices or biases.

I was crushed by the way the church had treated me. I believed that the reason I had lived when the other 11 fetuses my Mom conceived died was because God had a special ministry for me. When I entered the ministry and the three churches I served loved me, I felt that I was fulfilling that divine call.

But now the bottom was falling out. All that I loved in life was against me including the church. Over the years my faith was what had kept me afloat. With all the burdens I carried: feeling like a woman trapped in a man's body, two broken marriages, a developmentally disabled son, and alcohol addiction, I was able to bear it all knowing deep down that God loved me. Now I am told that because of my sin, God is ashamed of me and His love and forgiveness for me is on shaky ground. What is there left to live for? Over the next 4 months I again thought of suicide.

Chapter 8
Finding My True Self

I had tried so hard to be what society expected of me but I felt I had failed everyone – Daddy, Mom, my family, my friends, the church, Pam, and God. Intellectually I knew the Bible said God loved me and that Jesus died on the cross for me but emotionally I couldn't embrace it and His love.

I believe the central reason I couldn't embrace God's love was because of the church. I had always been taught that the church was God's 'spokesman in the world'. As Christian people living in a sinful world we naturally turn to the church for answers as to what is truth: Why did I do that? Can God forgive me? What should I do now? But now I have been rejected by the church and told that I am sick.

As long as I can remember I have gone to church. Church has been the rock of my life. With all the challenges I faced, I turned to the church for answers. My pastors have always reassured me of God's love and forgiveness. Now, I do not have that because "the church" says I am living in sin. Because of the church's condemning attitude, coupled with my belief that the church was God's 'spokesman in the world', I felt truly alone for the first time in my life. In November I sank to the bottom. With the compounding spiraling effect of my loneliness and belief that God no longer loved me, I revived the old suicide plan of slitting both wrists in a bathtub to contain the mess. Even though I valued other peoples' life, I didn't value mine anymore. The pain was too great to continue living any longer.

Christmas was really depressing. With the plans to commit suicide there was no joy in my heart. Christmas had always been my favorite time of the year but now it had no meaning – I was alone and the church had told me God's love was gone and the joy of Jesus' birth was not for me because of my sin.

I did not tell anyone that I was planning suicide. I knew if I did they would try to talk me out of it. I didn't want to be talked out of it. Yes, there were people I loved and I felt there were a handful of friends that loved me but that was not enough to stop me from doing it. I just wanted the pain to stop.

Then an amazing thing happened. One night in January of 2009 (after the New Year holiday), I had a dream. While sleeping I heard a voice in my head say, "Before you take your life why don't you go see a professional therapist and see if what the church told you was true. If it is true, then go ahead with your plans."

I believe to this day that voice in my head was God speaking to me and He knows me pretty well. He knows that if He told me directly not to do it I probably wouldn't have believed Him. I would have sloughed it off. But having me go to a professional therapist was different. He knew that my deepest hurt was centered on what the church had told me. So if the therapist could tell me they were wrong, well, that would not only stop me from doing the dastardly act but also give me great satisfaction. My pride would have been healed and my value as a person restored because right now my value as a person was at an all time low.

I searched the internet for a transsexual therapist near me in NC and found two. The first one I called was very friendly but said she no longer treated transsexuals. She highly recommended the other counselor, Dr. Lisa Griffin. I decided to call Dr. Griffin.

I called her and she immediately made me an appointment. I asked her how I should dress. She said to come dressed in the way that I was most comfortable. If that meant to come as Dawn then that was how I should come. I was starting to like her already.

I told Pam that I had made an appointment to see a therapist to find out what was wrong with me. I told her that I had severe gender identity issues and she agreed. She was happy I was going to see a therapist. I truly believe she was happy because she loved me and was happy that I was seeking help. I didn't deny that for I knew I truly needed it.

Dr. Griffin and I met for the first time April 2, 2009. As soon as I met her I knew that God didn't want me to go to the other counselor. He meant for me to see her. She immediately put me at ease. She was extremely professional. I never felt threatened or that I was being judged at any time during our conversation. As I told her my life story, I watched her face. Her look conveyed genuine care and interest. It was as if I was not just a client. She truly cared for me. I'm sure she could see the hurt I was experiencing.

I told her my life story and that never, to best of my knowledge, did I ever lust after a woman. I said I felt I never was a full blown man because I never got an erection when looking at a beautiful woman. Instead I always wanted to look like her. I desired for my body to look like her body. Then Dr. Griffin proceeded to talk to me about what being transgendered meant. She said transgendered is correctly used as an umbrella term for any gender dysphoria involving clothes of the opposite sex. That includes most commonly cross dressers (individuals who like to wear the clothes of the opposite sex but do not desire to have a sex change) and transsexuals (those individuals who believe they were born in the wrong body). It can also be used to refer to Gender Queer persons (those individuals who don't identify with one specific sex).

There are two kinds of recognized transsexuals: (1) those who are non-op, that is, just want to blend and live as the opposite sex but not have the physical surgery to remove their genitals and (2) those who desire to have surgery to make their bodies match who they feel they are inside. However, she said, today the term transgendered is frequently used synonymously with transsexual.

Her comments confirmed to me that I was indeed transgendered. Based on what she told me I figured I was a non-op transsexual, as I just wanted to be accepted as a woman, blend, and not have surgery.

She said I was not sick as the church had said. She said being a transsexual is not a choice as I was just being who I naturally was. In other words, I was wired that way and that's why I couldn't stop cross dressing. She also said it was remarkable that I had been able to suppress it for 51 years. It became clear to me that my feelings about wanting to commit suicide were because I had reached my limit of suppression. So I concluded I basically had two choices: embrace being transgendered and live or deny it and die as I would certainly kill myself within a short period of time.

Her non-judgmental advice meant so much to me, especially since she was Jewish. The scripture in Deuteronomy 22:5, part of the Torah and Jewish Law, is what the church was using to condemn me. It says, "A woman must not wear men's clothing, nor a man wear women's clothing for the Lord your God detests anyone who does this [NIV]". The King James Version (KJV) replaces the word 'detests' with 'abomination'. Yet here, a Jewish woman, who knows the Torah, was not using that scripture to condemn me like the United Methodist Church did. She saw me as a woman wearing women's clothing, not a man wearing women's clothing. Therefore, as a woman, I was not wearing clothes of the opposite sex but was wearing clothes of my true self.

All of this means that I do not fall under this condemnation. When I was in seminary at Duke I remembered learning that this law was directed mainly toward men and women who were wearing the clothes of the other gender for immoral reasons, sexual immorality, and so they could hide from punishment for crimes. This law was not directed toward people like me who genuinely felt like members of the other gender.

I had gone from the deepest depression, planning suicide to being glad to be alive. She had saved my life. She had made me see that God didn't hate me as He created me this way. I am who I am. Every person is unique as am I. She told me that being transgendered makes me very special, having experienced life on both sides. For the first time in my life I was happy with who I was.

When I left her office I was determined to pray about what she had told me. I felt pretty sure now that I wasn't offending God but I still wanted to talk to Him about it. While in prayer, my spirit told me the reason I lived and the other 11 fetuses aborted was because God had plans for me and those plans required that I had to go on the journey to womanhood. Now life sounded exciting! Instead of wanting to end my life, now I wanted to experience it to the fullest!

Within a month Dr. Griffin asked me to join a therapy group of transgendered women that she led at her home. She said the group included women in various stages of their journey and she felt it would be beneficial to me as it would provide a supportive environment for my transition to womanhood. I was thrilled for the opportunity and agreed to join.

I have been the therapy group for two years. During that time, the individual members of the group has changed, but the number has never exceeded 8 members at any given time for our 90 minute group session. Being able to help each other through sharing our experiences in a safe environment has been one of the main benefits. Dr. Griffin's central dynamic for the group was to provide support for us to come to understand how all of our 'parts' interact with each other and to come to understand ourselves better. During the time I was a member of the group, it definitely helped me to understand my 'parts' and to better interact with others. The group recently disbanded as it was time for us all to go our own way, i.e. out into the world and use what we had learned.

I grew close to a number of the members of the group. Four or five of us would regularly gather together and share dinner after our group session, enjoying the fellowship with each other. When the group disbanded we pledged to work hard at remaining in contact.

I left Dr. Griffin's office that day in April feeling exhilarated. I had now found my true self. I am, and have always been, a woman even though my body was born male. I had tried unsuccessfully to live in my biological gender for over 50 years. Now it was time to embrace who I truly am.

Chapter 9
Becoming a Woman

When I got home from my visit with Dr. Griffin my emotions were mixed. I was excited to know that I was not sick and that there was hope. I was excited that, with Dr. Griffins help, I could be the woman that I had always felt I was. But I was scared as I thought about what my decision would do to my marriage to Pam.

I have never felt gay as a male and never consciously was attracted to men when I was living as a man. For as long as I can remember, I have always been drawn to women. That part of my journey, the struggle of part of me trying to be a male (my biological sex) and part of me wanting to be a female has truly been a part of my life since my discovery when I was 8 years old. It is that continual struggle that finally wore me down and caused my emotional collapse after leaving the church.

I love Pam very much. Yes, I was initially attracted to her physical beauty as she is a very beautiful woman. But as I reflect, I realized that I am really more attracted to the inner beauty that she possesses. That is, I believe I was, and am still, attracted to her because she represents everything I want to be as a woman. She is a gentle, kind, compassionate, and loving woman that has a strong faith and loves God and Jesus very much. When deciding what to do, I prayed hard as I wanted so much for her to understand and support me but I was fearful she would not. I knew from the beginning that her family would not support me if I went through with the transition to a woman. I also knew I could live with their rejection but I didn't know if I could live with Pam's rejection. I had gone through one divorce with Shirley and had contemplated suicide then and I promised myself after that divorce that I would NEVER go through another divorce. But how could I avoid it if I transitioned? In my readings about transgendered people, I learned that 90% of transsexuals who go from Male to Female (M2F) lose their partners. The odds certainly were not in my favor but I knew if I didn't transition I probably would take my life anyway. It was a dilemma. What was I to do?

I decided that even with the fear of losing Pam I had to transition. I had been living a lie for over 50 years and I couldn't go on living that lie anymore. I had already lost one job (Methodist minister) because of it and would probably lose others. The desire to cross dress was so overwhelmingly strong I couldn't resist it anymore. The best solution to my dilemma was clearly to transition and put Pam in God's hands. I had to focus now on doing what was best for me and that was to transition. If I focused and worried too much about Pam and her reaction, I might let the fear of losing her force me to make the wrong decision. So I decided to start to live as a woman part-time.

That meant that I would go out as a woman in all public situations except work. I initially decided not to have SRS (Sex Reassignment Surgery). All I wanted was to blend – live and be accepted as a woman. I told that to Dr. Griffin and she supported me, writing me a Treatment Documentation letter to carry with me in case the police pulled me over for a road check while dressed as a woman. The letter stated that I was transgendered, living part-time as a woman and under her professional care with her phone number if they had any questions. I lived part-time from May 2009 until November 2010 with no problems.

As part of the process of living as a woman part-time, I had to start going out to public places dressed as a woman. I was scared so I contacted my hypnotist, Dawn Slavings, in Illinois. I emailed her with my concerns and her email reply said that I should start by going to a store, mingle down the aisles, pickup and look at some items, and then leave. That would get me used to being in a public place as a woman and would minimize putting me in any situation where I might fear detection. I thought about it and decided to go to a Walgreens Drug Store near home. It was close enough to home that I reasoned it was unlikely that anyone I knew would see me.

I dressed casually and went to the store. I went in, went down to the hair accessory aisle and picked up some hair bands. I was feeling good about everything and then it happened. A store clerk came up to me on my right side and said, "May I help you?" I was petrified. I quickly took an item off the rack, looked down so she couldn't see my face, and said, "No thank you. I'm just looking." She said okay and left. I took a breath, put the item back on the rack, turned and left the store. When I got into the car and closed the door, I almost cried. When the clerk asked me if she could help me, it was traumatic but then I realized that I passed. She took me for a woman and went about her business. Yes, I had passed!

Then I decided to get bolder. I decided to go to Hamrick's in Gaffney, SC and look at clothes. Why not? It was in South Carolina, another state, so the odds of someone seeing me there and recognizing me were quite remote. So I decided on the day and looked forward to my first shopping day as a woman.

I got dressed in a nice blouse and slacks with sandals and started down the road for the 45 minute drive to Gaffney, SC. Half way there I realized that I had to go to the bathroom real bad. While getting ready to go I had drunk a lot of tea and now I had to use the restroom. I became petrified – where can I go the bathroom? I certainly can't use the men's room dressed as a woman and I had never been in a ladies room before. I then decided I had to do the safest thing I could – I turned around and went back home.

When I got home I just made it to the bathroom in time. I took my female clothes off, disappointed that that my first shopping trip had failed. I called my hypnotist, Dawn Slavings, and talked to her about it. She immediately asked me, "Why didn't you just go to the ladies room at a gas station? They are run by people from Southeast Asia and they see a lot of transgendered people. They wouldn't have thought anything about it." I hadn't thought of that. We both laughed as I confessed that I guess I overreacted to the situation. From that day forward I had no problem using the ladies restroom and never was questioned. In fact, I passed with no hitches everywhere I went except for one situation in a restaurant in a mall north of my home town.

I went to the restaurant, by myself. Everything went fine until I was leaving. I saw a woman off in the distance who looked to me like she was waving. I waved back and said goodbye. She in turned said loudly so everyone in the restaurant could hear, "Thank you SIR". I'm sure I turned color as I left. When I got out the door the hostess came out and yelled out to me, "Ma'm'. I turned and, with tears in her eyes, she said, "I'm so sorry. Please come back." I told her thank you and left. I did not go back. When I shared the situation of being 'outed' (revealed in public that I was male) to a transgendered sister in my therapy group, she told me that the only time she was 'outed' was at the same restaurant inferring that someone there had a vendetta against transgendered people. Both of us are very passable so I don't know how she knew. My transgendered sister said she didn't go back to that restaurant either.

I talked with some of my transgendered sisters in therapy group about hormones and they said they felt so much better when they started. I wanted to go on hormones so badly but I kept talking myself out of it. I was afraid of the irreversible effects in case I decided, however unlikely, that I didn't like the way they made me feel or the changes they made in my appearance. I asked Dr. Griffin about my concerns and she said that after you start female hormones you can stop them up to 3 months after you start with no side effects and no permanent physical changes. After 3 months the changes are permanent and the only way back is through surgery.

So at 3 months you have to decide whether to continue or not. My fears went away after talking with her. Now I knew I had three months to choose so I decided to go ahead and start hormone therapy. I asked her to recommend a physician for an evaluation and prescription for estrogen. She sent me to Dr. Coles at Carolinas Medical Center where she had sent other M2F clients. I called Dr. Coles office and made an appointment to see her. When I went into her waiting room a peace and calmness came over me. I suddenly felt good about my decision to start hormone therapy and I wasn't a bit apprehensive. When she came into the examining room, she was very kind and had no trouble writing out the hormone prescription. When I left her office I IMMEDIATELY went to my drug store on West Franklin Boulevard in Gastonia, NC, and got it filled.

They knew I was transgendered there and all the staff was very professional and has always continually treated me with dignity. They support me in my journey and I continue to fill all my prescriptions there.

The prescription was for estradiol, a prescription form of estrogen. Unfortunately Pam's health insurance, that I was on, wouldn't cover it because I was a male, so I had to pay for it outright. I also got a prescription for an androgen inhibitor that blocks the production of testosterone. Since the androgen inhibitor is prescribed to treat prostate cancer, the insurance paid for it. That was okay. I didn't care. I was excited that I was on female hormones! I looked forward to taking my two 2 mg. pills twice a day. I took my first estradiol on May 14, 2009 and have been on them ever since.

I almost immediately felt its effect on my body and emotions. My body felt relaxed and good. My emotions were heightened and much more sensitive. I immediately noticed that I cried 'at the drop of a hat' especially when I watched movies and commercials on TV. I also had an uncontrollable urge to hold babies, I cried at weddings (even ones on TV), loved looking at toddler clothes in the store, thought baby animals were cute, didn't understand men, and loved to shop for clothes and jewelry.

I told Pam I was taking the hormones to see if I wanted to transition to be a woman. She supported me. Interestingly she told me later that when I decided to start hormones she knew I would continue on and transition to a woman. I didn't consciously know it but deep down I was thinking about going all the way then too.

I still put lipstick and earrings on when I drove to work. Except now I wore them into the building. I parked in the back and went upstairs via the back entrance so as to not draw attention to myself. Carrie, my supportive coworker, saw me and told me that I looked happy. I was happy. I was totally comfortable. I would take Kleenex with me when I talked to her so when I heard my supervisor come in through the back door, I would quickly wipe the lipstick off and pull the earrings off (they were clip-on) before he arrived. I hadn't told him yet and was not sure how he would react. I was fearful that it would cost me my job at the museum so I had to be careful. I was successful in this masquerade until that time I finally came out at work.

So when 3 months came and I had to decide if I wanted to keep taking the hormones, the decision wasn't hard. I felt so much at peace inside that I knew I wasn't going to stop. All of the feelings I felt was who I truly was. I knew that now I was at a point of no return. I decided to continue and the thought of irreversible changes didn't scare me. Instead I welcomed them. My feelings gave me the resolve to continue my journey to its completion. But now the question was how was I going to pay for Sex Reassignment Surgery (SRS)?

SRS was very expensive and insurance didn't cover the cost as they have always felt it was cosmetic and elective. They wouldn't cover any of it even with a letter from a doctor stating that a person's life depended on them having the surgery. I started praying about it and God sent me the answer – Daddy's inheritance money. When Daddy died, I ended up, after selling the house, car and getting his life insurance money, with about $150,000. I struggled with whether

Daddy would want me to use the money for the surgery. But I was reminded, as I prayed about it, that Daddy loved me and would want me to be happy so I decided to use it. Now all the pieces were in place except the doctor and a surgery date.

I wanted to celebrate my decision to have SRS and I knew the best way I could think of was to do something I have ALWAYS wanted to do – go to Glamour Shots. I checked online and found out that the Glamour Shots in Pineville, NC closed and the closest one was in Winston-Salem, a good 3 hour drive from Gastonia. I didn't care. I wanted to do it so I called and made an appointment in August of 2009. They said to bring three outfits (a dressy outfit, a casual outfit, and a sassy outfit). I knew which ones I would take. I got them and drove to Winston-Salem.

I was so excited I could hardly wait to get there. The 3 hour drive seemed like it took forever! Finally I made it to the Mall, parked the car, got the outfits, and walked into the Mall entrance. I looked around and couldn't find a directory so I went into one of the stores and asked them where Glamour Shots was. They said it was at the other end of the Mall (figures!). I said thanks, went back to the car, drove over to the other entrance, parked, and went back into the Mall. Right there by the entrance was Glamour Shots.

I walked in, told them who I was and that I had an appointment. They confirmed my appointment and took me back to the dressing rooms. In the section of the studio along the left side was the chairs and makeup counter where they did your makeup and on the right were rows and rows of clothes. I looked at the clothes and was glad I brought mine. They were better. They led me to the changing rooms and told me to put on my casual outfit. I entered and changed clothes.

When I got out of the changing room they directed me to the makeup counter and a man did my makeup. He really poured it on. I asked him if he was putting too much on and he said no as the camera would wash most of it out. When he had finished with me he took me back to the photography room where the pictures were taken.

I met my photographer and she was a doll. She was really sweet and very helpful. When she asked me to pose a certain way and I had trouble getting into the pose, she would help me move my body into the proper place. I wondered if she suspected I wasn't a woman since I couldn't get into those sexy poses naturally. She took a series of pictures and then said to go change into my dressy outfit.

I went back to the changing room and got into my black dress with pearls. I left there and went back to the photographic studio. She posed me again into some really neat poses including one where she had me pose on the edge of a mirror. She said that she got a picture of me and my reflection. She said when they developed it the picture of me would be in color and the reflection would be black and white. After she finished she said to go change into my sassy outfit. I was excited because I really liked my sassy outfit.

When I came out and back to the photography studio the photographer was amazed. My sassy outfit was a key-hole front go-go dress with yellow go-go boots. It was the outfit I was going to wear at the fund raising beauty pageant for Cornerstone that got cancelled. She took some really cool pictures with me in the go-go dress. She said that outfit was definitely her favorite. While arranging me in some poses I finally told her that I was having trouble because my body didn't naturally go into those poses as I was transgendered. She looked at me and smiled saying she suspected but said I looked very beautiful and made a very natural looking woman.

When she was done I went back into the changing room, got back into the clothes I wore to the Mall and went out to the monitor so I could see the pictures. When I looked at them I was amazed. I really looked good. I loved six of them and got a packet with those six which included one where I looked like Jamie Lee Curtis. When I left I felt wonderful and it was one more affirmation that I was really a woman.

Since I was going 'all the way', I decided to go on July 17, 2009 and get my ears pierced. Clip-on earrings were hurting my ears and there were so many more choices with pierced earrings. I decided to go to Claire's at South Park Mall in Charlotte, North Carolina. There was a Claire's at the local mall but again, I felt more comfortable going to a store where it was less likely someone I knew would see me dressed as a woman. Besides, my hometown of Gastonia, NC was very homophobic.

When I told the 20 something clerk I wanted my ears pierced she asked me for my driver's license. I didn't understand. I asked her, "Why do I need to show you my driver's license? I'm an adult." I panicked because my driver's license had a male picture and male name and I was dressed as a woman. She said it was company policy. I gave her my driver's license and I gave her Dr. Griffin's Treatment Documentation letter explaining I was transitioning to a woman. I felt that was the safest way of explaining my situation without causing a commotion. I handed her my driver's license and the letter at the same time. When I gave her the letter, she asked me, 'Why the letter?" I smiled and told her I was transgendered and that's why my driver's license shows a male picture and name. She smiled back and said she understood and gave them both back to me. She then proceeded to pierce my ears with gold ball studs.

While she pierced my ears we talked about my journey. During the discussion she asked me why I chose to transition. I told her because I had always felt like a woman from the time I was eight. She told me she knew a few transgendered women and she believed that everyone had the right to live their lives as they saw fit as long as it didn't physically hurt anyone. I agreed. After she finished putting the gold studs in my ears we stood and talked for another 10 minutes about my journey. She was very supportive.

After I had it done I wondered why I had waited so long. It wasn't anything big and it made me feel so good! Since my discovery at Grandma's house with her earrings, I have always had a fascination with earrings and felt they were a strong sign of femininity. Even though women predominantly wear earrings, many guys today wear them too so I felt I could wear the piercing studs (and later small hoops) at work and not be noticed. I know now that my feeling good inside after having my ears pierced was a strong affirmation on the outside of how I felt inside, that is, that I am a woman. It was one more important step in my journey to womanhood.

I knew the transition was progressing pretty fast so I decided to take Pam to Linville Falls on the Blue Ridge Parkway over Labor Day of 2009. I wanted this trip to Linville Falls, one our favorite places to visit, to be a special time. I wanted so much for us to enjoy being together as husband and wife, maybe for the last time. I dressed in blue jeans, a tee shirt and wore no jewelry or anything that would shout 'girl'. However we soon found out that my plans were not going to happen as it became apparent, early on, that my transition had gone too far for us to be seen as husband and wife.

On the way to Linville Falls, I needed to go the bathroom. We stopped at a Burger King so I could use the restroom. I went in to the men's restroom thinking that was where I should go as I was dressed in male clothes. As soon as I entered, a man, who was leaving looked at me and I could read in his eyes, "What are you doing in the men's room? You're a woman." I went ahead and used the restroom but little did I know that this was going to be the first of many indications that I was now seen as a woman.

While on the Blue Ridge Parkway on the way to Linville Falls, Pam and I stopped at a roadside picnic area to share the lunch that we had packed. While there we noticed a van that had pulled in to the parking area. The couple rolled down their window and called out to us for some help. We went over to see what they wanted. They were lost and wanted directions to Linville Falls. We obliged and told them how to get there. They thanked us and left.

We went back to our lunch, leisurely enjoying our time together and the beautiful scenery. After finishing, Pam and I proceeded to Linville Falls. We expected a lot of cars there as it was a beautiful day. We went to the Upper Falls trailhead behind the Parkway store and started up the trail. As we were climbing up the trail, who should we meet coming down the trail but the couple we gave the directions to. They apparently had gotten there before us. They stopped and talked with us for a few moments and as we turned to leave the wife turned, and with a smile said, "Hang in there ladies. You're almost there." I looked at Pam and she looked at me. I told her that I wasn't deliberately trying to present myself as a woman. I had done all I could to present as a male. She looked at my chest and said, "Your breasts gave you away." I looked down and had to agree with her. They definitely stood out even without a bra.

We went on up to the upper falls, enjoying looking at the wildflowers on the side of the trail. When we got back to the parking lot I told Pam I had to use the restroom. I looked at her and said that considering that the woman on the trail considered me a woman, I'd better use the ladies room. Pam agreed. However, when I went to the ladies room door it was closed because of no water. Pam then said we could go back to the main Blue Ridge Parkway road and over to the Linville Falls Picnic Area and use the restrooms there.

We drove into the Picnic Area and found the restrooms. I got out and, as we discussed earlier, went into the Ladies Room. When I exited the stall, there was a mother with her 8-10 year old daughter washing their hands. I waited until they were done and proceeded to wash mine. While washing my hands she turned and talked to me like any other woman in the restroom. She left, I finished, and then I returned to my car. When I got into the car, Pam looked at me and asked me if I had any problems. I said none. I told her that I was totally accepted as a woman. She smiled and said, "I told you so."

When Pam and I returned to Gastonia I held her, cried and apologized. I told her I wanted this to be our day together as husband and wife. She said she knew that and that it was okay. She said it was apparent that those days were now gone. I was a woman now and there was no way to hide it.

By September 2009 it was getting very difficult to hide my physical changes at work. My breasts were now a C cup and I wasn't able to hide them very well. My deportment also was changing. I had a definite sway in my hips when I walked when I wasn't even trying.

My co-worker Carrie was telling me every few days that women at work were asking her, "What's wrong with Duane? Does he have breasts? He's acting and looking like a woman." Carrie told me, "You can't hide it anymore. The changes are too obvious now. You have to come out." I looked at her and agreed so I made plans.

I consulted various books (as well as talked to my therapist) on transitioning at work and they all recommended telling your supervisor in private and writing a letter to your co-workers explaining why you are transitioning. I made an appointment to meet with the Museum Director and my supervisor.

I told both of them that I was transitioning to become a woman and I was pleased to hear them both say that they supported me completely. Interestingly, I asked the Director if she knew and she said yes. I then turned to my boss and asked him if he knew and he said he had no idea. The Director tugged at my arm, smiled and said to me as one woman would say to another woman, "Men are so clueless." I immediately smiled back. That was a moment that I will never forget as it was the first time where I not only was accepted as a woman but was related to as a woman.

We all decided that I should write a letter explaining why I was transitioning and the Director said she would write a supportive letter and attach her letter to mine. We had tossed around the idea of sending them both to everyone via email but decided against it as it would potentially be accessible to all city employees. It was determined that the Director would put both letters in everyone's museum mailbox at the end of the day on Thursday, November 12. I would take Friday, November 13 off, allowing everyone time to read the letters. I would then return to work, Monday, November 16, 2009, as Dawn.

The following is the letter that I wrote explaining my transition:

"As you probably have noticed, my appearance has been changing lately. There is a reason for that.

I have had gender identity issues since I was 8 years old. I have been hiding them for fear of being ridiculed and misunderstood. I know I cannot continue living as I have been living. For that reason I have been seeing a therapist since March of 2009 and have been diagnosed transgendered. I am now in transition to become a woman. That is the reason for the changes in my appearance. I will be living full time, at the Museum, as a woman from now on.

My new name is Dawn. Please try to refer to me by my new female name and use female pronouns in reference to me. I know you will forget and it will take time to learn. All I ask is that you try.

I know many of you will have questions and desire to understand things better. Know that I am completely understanding of your feelings and my door is always open to talk. Please try to understand my reasons for these changes. Even though the outside package is changing I am still the same caring and compassionate person on the inside. I am not making these changes for any reason other than to make my outer appearance agree with my inner gender. Also, know that I will continue to do all my duties, as an employee of the Schiele Museum, with the level of professionalism that I have always done as it relates to you and the public.

Pam knows of these changes and is understanding and supportive. She wants the best for me and knows that these changes are needed for my wellbeing. It is my prayer you will also feel the same way and support me in this transition.

Dawn (Duane) Flynn"

After I gave a copy of my letter to the Museum Director, she in turn sent a copy to the City of Gastonia City Manager, the City Attorney, and the City Human Resources Manager so they knew what was happening and to be sure that the Museum was handling it properly. The Museum Director told me later that the response from the City was total support and that the City Attorney was very impressed with the openness of my letter. I also found out later that I am the first, as far as the City of Gastonia records indicate, transgendered employee in their 100+ year history.

I was somewhat nervous when I came to work as Dawn on that Monday, November 16th, but less so than I originally thought I would be. As it turned out, everyone was supportive except for 4 co-workers (out of 40). Those four included two women and two men. The men were 'good ole Southern Baptist boys' who just couldn't understand why a man would want to be a woman. One of the women was a receptionist and the other was up in Administration. Overall I was very pleased with everyone's acceptance.

The receptionist that didn't support it, I found out later, said she "did not want *him* to be allowed in the women's bathroom she would be using". To placate her concerns, Administration requested I use a designated restroom (a single bathroom with a lock on the door) in the Education wing of the building until I had my sex change surgery. I agreed. It was inconvenient but it was the best solution to the problem. Restroom use is a common problem for pre-op transgendered women. Some women still see transgendered women as men and feel uncomfortable with them sharing their bathroom. Many times this causes significant inconvenience. I know of a transgendered sister who had to go three floors up from her work environment to use the restroom until she had her surgery.

Today, two of the other unsupportive co-workers have left (the woman who had the bathroom issue was laid off and one of the men retired). I found out later that the other man really didn't have trouble with my transition. The problem was with a misunderstanding between him and his supervisor regarding how he looked at me in the hallway. His supervisor was the man who retired so when he got a new supervisor the misunderstanding was cleared up and he was fine. The other female, the one in Administration, will never accept me as she used to be one of my parishioners and it is too much for her to accept that her pastor did this. That's okay. She still does her professional responsibilities regarding my records for which I am grateful. We just don't talk anymore. I miss the friendship we had before I transitioned but I have come to accept that it's her problem and not mine. If she ever wants to talk, I will be there to welcome her.

I needed to tell my sons about the transition. I dreaded telling them as I feared the worst. Again I consulted various books and talked to my therapist about the best way to go about it. After gathering all the ideas I decided to write Andrew a letter. Due to the emotional nature of telling family, it is recommended that you sit down and write a letter, telling them everything the way you want to tell them. Usually when transgendered people tell someone directly, the emotion of the moment most frequently causes them to forget what they want to say. For that reason it is recommended that you tell them in a carefully crafted letter and then talk to them after they have had time to read and digest it.

I wrote the following letter to Andrew and sent it to him in mid-December 2009:

Dear Son,

As I write this letter to you, I hope you and Veronica are doing well. It seems like it was years ago that you were here and we went to the coin show in October. How time flies! As you get older I'm sure you will find that to be true more.

Son, this is a very difficult letter for me to write you. It is going to contain information that is going to shock you. It will no doubt cause you much pain and for that I am so very sorry. There is nothing I would ever do to deliberately hurt you or cause you pain but this cannot be avoided. As you read this letter please remember that I love you with all my heart and that love will never cease regardless of how you feel about what I am going to tell you.

I'm sure you remember that I elected to leave the ministry in the Methodist church about a year and half ago. After I left the church in July of last year I went through a terrible time of depression. The church had beaten me up so bad that I had lost much of my will to live. I had even considered suicide in November. As I struggled with my depression I came to understand, inside of me, that there was something more serious going on than I wanted to face. And I knew I needed professional help to find out what it was. So in February of this year I went to a professional therapist for an evaluation. She was highly recommended and I was hopeful I could get some answers. Through our discussion together it became clear what my problem was – I am transgendered.

Please, son, don't throw the letter down. Please allow me to tell you the rest of the story.

I listened to her and tried to keep an open mind. Everything she told me made sense. It was clear to me that my refusal to accept being transgendered was why I wanted to end my life. I had suppressed it for over 50 years and had lived in terror of rejection by loved ones. It had become so unbearable that I couldn't face life anymore. She told me that the only way I would be happy would be to embrace it, that is, accept it. I knew that if I didn't I could end up harming myself. So I embraced it. Last May I went to a physician, started hormones, and as of Monday, Nov. 16th, have been living full time as a woman named Dawn.

You don't know much about my childhood. As a child I always struggled with gender identity. I had felt like a girl for as long as I can remember. Just playing, I once tried on a pair of Grandma Flynn's clip-on earrings when I was eight. When I put them on it was more than make believe. I remember it felt right. I knew from then on that I was different. For fear of rejection from family and friends I hid it. When your Grandma Helen was visiting neighbors, I cross dressed.

She never knew. I cross dressed whenever I could – all through school, college, and even while I was married to your mother. I kept trying to suppress it and hide it. My church upbringing kept making me feel guilty. I was forever afraid God couldn't love me. But the more I tried to stop, the more I felt the need. I threw away a number of piles of clothes trying to stop, only to later buy more. If you have read anything about transgendered people, you will understand my behavior.

*It is now known that being transgendered **is not a choice**. All human embryos, when conceived, are female. Only later does the embryo differentiate as whether it will be male or stay female. Medicine has found that with transgendered people that the differentiation is not clearly defined.*

My choice to live as a woman has become one that impinges heavily on my health. Most people can't believe I have kept it buried for over 50 years. Most transgendered people can't keep it 'under wraps' for more than a few years. So, now maybe you can understand why my health depended on me embracing it.

All my professional contacts, coworkers, and true friends accept me as Dawn and embrace me. They love me and know that I am the same caring, compassionate person. The outside wrapping has just changed. I am not out to make a statement to the world. All I want is to blend. All I want is to be free to go out in public as a woman, pass as a woman, and be accepted as a woman.

The hormones have done well and passing is not a problem. I pass with no problems in all situations. I have been shopping at various malls, gone to many restaurants, and talked to people two feet from me and all accept me as the woman I am. Since I blend as a woman I have no plans to have SRS (Sex Reassignment Surgery) at this time.

I still love Pam with all my heart. I always will. We both recognize we are soul mates and don't want to live without each other so we are trying to find a way to make this work. It is very hard for Pam so remember her in your thoughts. I am trying very hard to do all I can to ease her adjustment and reaffirm my love to her daily. Only time will tell whether we will be able to find a way to make it work.

So, I am happy son. I am at real peace for the first time in my life. I hope you have stayed with me and have read the whole letter. I want you to know it is okay if you are angry. I would expect that. But remember, no matter how you feel about me, I will always love you. Understand I do not ever want to be your mother. You have only one mother. I know it will be hard to look at me as your father when I am dressed as a woman and I do not expect you to address me as dad. You can address me as Dawn.

After you have had time to think about all this, please either call me or email me. I so much want to hear from you one way or the other. Remember, I will always love you and I hope that you will always love me.

All my love forever

Dawn

I waited for about a week and never got a phone call, email, or letter. I got worried that I had lost him. I prayed frequently, asking God to intervene and soften his heart and to prepare me for the worst. Then, while on the phone on another call (where I was placing a cosmetic order with an Avon Lady at church), I heard a beep telling me I had a voice mail. When I listened to the voice mail I was shocked. It was Andrew and he said he got my letter and that he definitely wanted to talk. Most importantly his voice was calm and full of compassion. After I stopped crying I called him.

When he answered the phone he said he was glad I called. He said, first of all, that he wanted me to know that he loved me, I was family, and that would never change. Then he said, "Yes, I'm upset." I thought, 'Oh boy. Now it's coming'. But what he said blew me away. He said, "Yes I'm upset. I'm upset that you had to suffer for so long before you decided to transition." I started to cry and cried for about 15 seconds without stopping. I couldn't believe what I heard. My son was accepting my transition and still loved me. It was a definite answer to my prayers. He said he told Veronica (his fiancée) and her 18 year old daughter and they totally supported me. He asked me what he should call me for he obviously couldn't call me Dad anymore. I said I didn't want him to call me Mom as he only has one mother and she alone deserves to be called Mom. I told him to call me Dawn. He said he was okay with that. He then said that they wanted to see me and Pam after the New Year. Pam and I agreed and we planned to go see him and Veronica the first weekend in January 2010.

All the way down to Atlanta I kept replaying my conversation with Andrew on the phone. I kept telling myself that he said he loved me and it didn't matter. It just all seemed too good to be sure. I told Pam when we got there to be prepared for the shock of seeing me as a woman may change his mind. When we walked in the house, he came up to me, hugged me, and told me he loved me. My fears were quickly put to rest. As Andrew had said, all three of them were very open, kind, and supportive.

During our stay we all went to the Art Museum and the Coca Cola Museum in Atlanta. We all had a great time with no hitches in public or with each other. On the way home Pam and I were amazed that during the whole time we were there, Andrew, Veronica, and her daughter never called me by my male name and never used male pronouns. It was as if I had always been Dawn. It was amazing! My son, my closest relative next to Pam, saw that my transition was natural and felt my peace and happiness. The whole experience was very affirming of my decision to transition.

I also had to tell Davy, which concerned me as he was non-verbal and therefore couldn't read so I couldn't send him a letter like I did Andrew. The first time I went to visit him as Dawn he held my hand (he's always been a lady's man) but he kept looking at me like he knew something was different but he couldn't quite figure it out. I didn't push it. I left him that day understanding that it was a lot for him to try to understand at one time.

The next time I went to see him I decided to put it in God's hands and one way or another, I was going to tell him. When I got him I put him in a wheel chair and we went out to one of the decks at his dormitory. He usually talked (babbled) when I got him but that day he was quiet. After I put him next to a bench and before I sat down, I took my jewelry off (he likes to grab jewelry and yank it off). I pulled him next to me, with each of us facing each other. Shortly after I positioned him, he grabbed my head (he is very strong) and pulled our cheeks together so his right cheek was against my right cheek. He held me there for a good two minutes. Neither one of us said a thing. During that time I felt him tell me, through our connected cheeks, "It is okay. I understand." After he let go he smiled and started babbling. It was like we were old friends. We stayed out on the deck for the better part of an hour. Davy was clearly happy and very comfortable with me. I knew in my heart that what I felt when our cheeks were touching was real and that he truly knew who I was and was totally okay with it. I have never been so touched in my whole life. It was the most amazing feeling I have ever felt. God clearly let me know he understood and I need not worry about it. From that point on Davy and I have been fine and the joy we share continues to grow each time I visit.

After coming out full time I decided that I needed to go shopping and start building a new wardrobe. I asked my dear friend and co-worker, Carrie, if she would go with me. She agreed and we decided to go to South Park Mall in Charlotte. We had such a great time together. We went to Macy's and I bought my first purse. It was brown with light brown patches. While at Macy's I wanted to get my first makeover. I went to the Este Lauder counter as I knew that Este Lauder was a widely recognized high end cosmetic company. The lady who did makeovers was not there but would be back within an hour. Carrie and I went shopping in other stores in the mall where I bought some underwear and some shoes. We returned to Macy's and the cosmetician was there. She took my makeup off and I feared she would see my beard stubble and say something but she didn't. She was kind and treated me like she would any other woman.

When she was done I bought some of the makeup and gave her a $10 tip. She looked at me with shock on her face. She said no one had ever tipped her before. I told her she deserved it and proceeded to tell her I was transgendered. She smiled and said she suspected when she took my makeup off but said I really did look good. She then told me about someone else she knew that was transgendered and she admired them for doing what they felt was right. When we left I had not only gotten some much needed makeup and clothes, but I had gotten a makeover and found that not everyone is prejudiced against transgendered people.

On January 8, 2010, I got a new Treatment Documentation letter from Dr. Griffin stating that I was in the process of changing my personal identify from male to female and was living full time in the female role. It was comforting to have the letter even though I never needed to use it. I have been very blessed in that I have always had soft features and build so that, except for the one time noted earlier, I have never been questioned.

In early 2010 I met with Dr. Griffin in a private therapy session. In it she told me, "Dawn, you need to go back to church. Church is a very important part of your life." I agreed but I was afraid to go back. I was afraid I would be struck down like Ananias and Sapphira in Acts 5 because of my 'sin' that the church said I was committing. She reassured me that would not happen. I fervently prayed about it and realized she was right. I decided to find a church.

I sent an email to Dr. Griffin asking her for a list of LGBTQI (Lesbian, Gay, Bisexual, Transgendered, Queer, Intersex) friendly churches in Charlotte for I knew there were none in my home town of Gastonia.

She sent me a list. I decided to check out the first church on the list – a Unitarian Universalist Church.

I went and, as Dr. Griffin had said, I was not struck down. Being a seminary graduate from Duke, I found the service interesting. The ministers brought into the sermon universal truths that are present in all world religions. They tied them together in such a way as to not affirm any one religion. After the service, I stopped for coffee in the Fellowship Hall and met a wonderful racially mixed couple.

They told me that they came to the Unitarian Universalist Church because they were rejected by their local church since they were racially mixed. I told them I was also rejected by my local church because I was transgendered. They were totally accepting and we became great friends.

After the three of us had attended there for about three weeks we all decided to attend a new member class after worship one Sunday. I was seriously considering joining as they were a strong LGBTQI affirming church and I felt comfortable there. The only element of the church, at this point, that was negative was its size. The services were large (around 300 people) and it was hard to get to know anyone.

In the class a member of the church explained all about the church's history and its programs. I listened intently but noticed that not much about Christian programs was mentioned. When I asked the moderator about it, he gave me a quizzical look and said, "People that attend here that were once Christians come here to get away from church ritualism and programs so they (the Unitarian Universalist Church) did not have any Christian programs except a small Sunday school before worship."

My friends looked at me and saw my countenance fall. I was very disappointed. I liked the church but I had to have more than just a Sunday school. I needed communion. They got up and left. I stayed until the end of the session and when I went out the door, my friends hollered at me. They were over to the side and had waited for me to come out. They were writing a note inviting me to come with them to a church the next Sunday that they thought I would like, Metropolitan Community Church of Charlotte. They said they had attended and they liked it very much. They said it practiced Christian worship with communion every Sunday and was LGBTQI affirming. With excitement in my soul, I agreed to meet them there next Sunday.

I got there early before my friends arrived. I always leave from home early when I go to new places as I want to be sure to leave enough time to get there in case I get lost. The Unitarian Universalist Church was not what I would identify as a true Christian church as it did not practice traditional Christian worship with baptisms and communion. So, the more I thought of it, my 'lack of being struck down by God' really did not apply there. So I got nervous all over again. This new church was truly a Christian church therefore the fears came back. Was I going to be struck down when I walked in the door? Well, I decided it didn't really matter. Dr. Griffin was right. I needed to be back in church so I resolved that if I died when I walked in, at least I died in church.

When I walked in the front door a very kind gentleman named Gary met me there. He was able to see my apprehension (either it was very obvious or the Lord opened his eyes). He came over, gave me a big hug, welcomed me, and sat with me until my friends arrived. Immediately my fears went away. And yes, there was no fire or lightning from heaven. When my friends got there we went into worship. The worship was more than I ever expected. It was very uplifting, affirming, and I felt God put His arms around me and tell me, "Dawn, I love you just the way you are." I cried and from that moment on I knew that all would be well because I had now come back home.

Some of you may ask, 'How did you know it was God who put His arm around you and not Satan tricking you into believing all was okay?' I was slain in the Spirit three times in 1995. I have gifts of the Spirit including speaking in tongues and healing. I know God's Spirit lives within me because I have seen these gifts manifested in my life. And I know that Satan and God can't coexist in the same place at the same time. So if God's Spirit lives within me then Satan's spirit can't reside there at the same time. That's how I know.

Pam was becoming more and more uncomfortable with my transition. I was living full time now and I was unmistakably a woman. In March, 2010 she told me, "You are clearly a woman now. I am straight and can't live with a woman so one of us has to leave." I voluntarily left, leaving her to stay in the house. I got a one bedroom apartment in town. On March 17, 2012 I moved from the one bedroom apartment to a two bedroom in the same apartment complex and am living there today. I was okay with moving out as I felt it was best to give Pam space to adjust. I hoped that she would eventually come around and invite me back home because I knew in my heart that she still loved me.

To assist in my transition I decided to visit a high-end cosmetic store, Sephora, at Northlake Mall not far from my home. I had done a lot of reading of periodical magazines like Cosmopolitan and Glamour, especially the cosmetics sections. I experimented at home to find a look that was natural and not overdone and felt I had done well but I wanted to learn more. Yet I was still nervous, fearful of being discovered as they would have to remove all my makeup to do a makeover.

My fears were unfounded as I was quickly put at ease by the sales representative who met me. Her name was Bea. She proceeded to answer my questions, give me a makeover and make me feel beautiful. She was so kind I felt safe in revealing myself to her. When I told her I was transgendered she smiled and reassured me it was fine. She complimented me on my appearance and deportment which made me feel even more beautiful.

I visited the store many times after that (and still do to this day) and have met another supportive sales representative, Anne. Both women gave me a very special gift – the gift of unconditional acceptance. They both love me as a person and accept me as the woman I am.

I have had trouble with getting my driver's license changed since going full time as a female. I had legally changed my name to Dawn Jennifer Flynn on January 5, 2009. I went a few weeks later to a NC Driver's License Bureau in Lincolnton, NC (on a recommendation from a transgendered friend who said they were kind to him) to get a new driver's license with my new name, a new picture, and new gender marker. The examiner was extremely cruel to me. He changed my name (since I had the documentation from the court) and took my picture but said in a loud voice so all in the room could hear, "I am not going to change your gender marker until you show me a letter from the doctor saying it's been cut off". He looked like an ex-Marine Sergeant who had a vendetta against people he felt were homosexual (which I wasn't). He did all he could to embarrass me as he put my male middle name, James, with my female first name on my license.

When I told him my middle name was Jennifer not James, he glared at me and said, "I suppose you want me to change it?" I said, "I do". He changed it but continued to glare at me. When I got the new license with female picture, female name, and male gender marker I turned to him, smiled, said, "Thank you" and left. I didn't say a mean word to him during the whole situation. I was determined to be a lady no matter what. When I got out into the car I cried like a baby. I was deeply hurt by his actions. I started to have doubts as to whether I would be able to withstand the abuse I was going to face in the homophobic cities I lived and shopped in.

I found out that NC law said that in order to get ones gender marker legally changed on your driver's license you needed to (1) have documentation of a legal name change (which I had) and (2) have the minimum of top surgery. For F2M (female to male) it meant breast reduction surgery. For M2F (male to female) it meant breast augmentation. In everyday life, your driver's license is your key means of identification. Every time you use a charge card you have to show your driver's license and I use charge cards a lot. I got tired of having to explain its inconsistencies (male gender maker) and everyone standing in line finding out I was transgendered. When I finished explaining to the clerk that I was transgendered and was in transition to becoming a woman, got my items, and turned to leave, I got so many stares and heard so many hurting remarks that I decided to go ahead and have breast augmentation so I could get my driver's license gender marker changed.

I got the name of the plastic surgeon two of my transgendered sisters used and contacted him (Dr. Jean Pierre Riou in Cornelius, NC). They said he was the best and highly recommended him. I called his office and made an appointment as soon as possible. When I met him I was immediately put at ease. After I told him I was transgendered he asked me what size I wanted. I told him I didn't want huge breasts. I just wanted enough to get my driver's license gender marker changed and enough to be able to show some cleavage. We talked and agreed on what I needed (I was a C cup just from the hormones so we decided to just increase it to a D cup and that would give me some cleavage). We set the surgery date for July 2, 2010. He wrote me a letter for the driver's license bureau stating that I was in transition, had breast augmentation surgery date set, and told them to change my gender marker from male to female.

I went to a different Driver's License Bureau on a recommendation from a different friend (the one in Mt. Holly, NC) who said they were nice. When I got to an examiners table I showed them the letter Dr. Riou wrote. The female examiner took the letter to a male examiner who I assume was the lead examiner. They talked briefly and she returned. She said that they would not change my gender marker until the surgery was done. Having it scheduled was not enough. I proceeded out to the car, shut and locked the doors, and cried for 10 minutes. I was crushed. I wanted to end the ridicule so badly. It seemed to me that the world was against anyone who was transgendered. It was almost like they were deliberately making everything so difficult that the transgendered person would give up and change their mind. Well, I wasn't going to change my mind. I just accepted that I was going to go ahead with the augmentation surgery and try again after it healed.

I had the surgery July 2, 2010. Even though I didn't really need the surgery as I was happy with C cup breasts, I was actually looking forward to the surgery. Not only would it finally fulfill all the stupid requirements of the state of NC to get my gender marker changed but it would make me look better and consequently make me feel better about myself. I had a girlfriend, Tricia, take me for the surgery. Dr. Riou did the surgery in the clinic attached to his office. Tricia drove me to the clinic at about 10am. They took me and prepared me for the surgery. The surgery was scheduled for around 11am. I don't remember anything about it except Tricia and Dr. Riou holding me up after the surgery and walking me to the car which was parked at the loading dock in the back of the clinic. After I got into the car Tricia proceeded to get lost trying to get home (this trip to the clinic was her first). I remember fighting to stay awake so I could direct her on how to get back to my apartment. When we got back I remember Tricia wasn't strong enough to get me into the apartment. She told me later that she asked my neighbor to help. The two of them helped me walk to my bed.

After getting home I don't remember anything for the rest of that day or the night. Tricia told me later that I moaned and complained constantly that I was in pain. I had told her before the surgery that I had a high tolerance for pain and yet she said I didn't seem to be handling the pain well. She said she called the Doctor's office and asked them for advice. Being the dear friend she was, she stayed with me all night, taking care of all my needs. The next day I was 'together' enough that she was able to go home.

I was bandaged completely around my chest from just below my neck almost to my belly button. My chest was really sore (obviously) from the surgery. I was told that I could not take the bandage off for 2-3 weeks. Dr. Riou had told me during my initial visit that after the bandage is removed I could only wear sports bras for a month. Fortunately I had purchased a couple before the surgery. I faithfully used only the sports bras for about 3 weeks during which time I went to Belks and bought some D cup bras. When I was able to go back to regular bras it felt so good to finally have some support. Sports bras don't give much support but I understand why I needed to wear them at the beginning because they were not restrictive. When I removed the bandage I immediately saw the area between and below my breasts. It was a beautiful blue and black where it bruised during the surgery. I remember Dr. Riou saying that it would go away in a couple weeks. He was right. It went away after about another two weeks and then everything looked like I had been born with D cup breasts! They were gorgeous.

I went back to Dr. Riou and got a new letter stating the surgery had been completed and took it to a third Driver's License Bureau, this time in my home town of Gastonia, NC. Tricia went with me in case I lost my temper if they refused a third time. However, when I told the Examiner why I was there and he looked at the letter from Dr. Riou, he said, "No problem". He made the necessary changes and ordered my new Driver's License. I almost cried on the spot. Tricia grabbed my arm and let me lean over onto her shoulder to lightly sob for joy. The examiner filled out the necessary paper work, I signed it and we were done. I shook his hand and thanked him verbally and with my eyes. He looked at me and said, "You are very welcome" and we left. When we got to the car I proceeded to really cry for joy. My gender marker was finally changed!

The examiner was very kind and treated me with respect, unlike the other Examiners. I was so pleased with the experience that I wrote a letter of commendation to the Commissioner in Raleigh, NC, commending his professionalism.

Chapter 10
The Final Step

After living as a woman for a few months, full time, it dawned on me (no pun intended) that I may as well have SRS. If I was going to live full time as a woman I needed to truly be a woman. Otherwise my life would be a lie and I didn't want to lie anymore. I started asking everyone I knew if I needed FFS (Facial Feminization Surgery) and, with no exceptions, all said my facial features were soft enough and that I didn't need it. So I decided to not have FFS. My face would remain my own. So I pursued where to have my SRS.

I talked with a transgendered sister, Paige, about where to go for my SRS. She had gone to Dr. Pierre Brassard in Montreal, Canada, and had a wonderful experience. After listening to her experience, I decided that was where I also wanted to go. Now I feared that I wouldn't be accepted as he was considered one of the best in the world. I went online and requested an application. I received it within a couple weeks and filled it out within a couple hours. It required a letter from my therapist and a counselor affirming that, in their professional opinion, I was a candidate for SRS. My therapist, Dr. Griffin, said she would be happy to draft a letter of recommendation and she said she would recommend a counselor to go to for my second letter.

I called Dr. Griffin's recommended counselor, Rev. Jim Greene, a licensed counselor who had experience counseling transgendered candidates for SRS, for my second letter. His office was in Charlotte and he said he would be happy to see me. He said it would take two sessions of one hour each. I agreed and made the appointments (May 24 and May 28, 2010). After the two sessions he agreed to write me a letter of recommendation for SRS, dating the letter May 28. Dr. Griffin gave me her letter dated May 24. Both letters stated that, in their professional opinions, based on the standards set by the World Professional Association for Transgender Health (WPATH) Standards of Care for Gender Identity Disorders, that I was an appropriate candidate for Sex Reassignment Surgery. These two letters were the validation of who I have always felt I was. Reading their recommendations brought me great joy.

I sent my application on June 18, 2010 to Dr. Brassard for my SRS. Included in the application were my two letters recommending SRS from Dr. Griffin and the Rev. Jim Greene, along with a letter from Dr. Obi, my endocrinologist, stating that I was on estrogen therapy, under his care, since May 14 (I had been under the care of another doctor, Dr. Coles, previously from May 2009).

In the two letters were statements that I had lived full time in my new gender role (female) since November 16, 2009. This also met the requirements of the World Professional Association for Transgender Health (WPATH) Standards of Care for Gender Identity Disorders for sex reassignment surgery which state you have to live in your new gender role full time for a year before you can undergo SRS.

I got an email back within a couple weeks stating that I was accepted for Sex Reassignment Surgery on January 11, 2011. After I was accepted for SRS in Montreal, I needed to get my passport changed and send the first surgery payment.

Dr. Brassard asked that the surgery costs ($18,000 Canadian) be sent in three payments (1st: $2,000 by October 15; 2nd: $2,500 by November 15; 3rd: balance by December 11). Along with each payment due by a certain date, certain pre-surgery tests were also due by those dates. Initialized copies of the letter of confirmation and packing list (the documents that came in first shipment) by October 15. Nothing additional was due with the second payment on November 15. Laboratory test results and travel information documents were due with the third payment on December 11.

I shipped each of my certified checks via UPS to insure them if they got lost. After I shipped the check I notified Dr. Brassard's office via email that the payment (and other requested paperwork) was on its way.

My first two payments were received okay but there were problems with the third payment of $13,507.65. I sent it via UPS on December 2nd but one of the women in the office lost it. After much sharing of emails it became apparent that I needed to send another check. But I also had to cancel the other check in case someone found it somewhere. I went to my bank and had them cut another certified check for $13,507.65 and shipped it to Montreal. But when I asked to cancel the other certified check I found out that is very hard to do.

In order to cancel a certified check: (1) I had to fill out an Application for Lost Cashier's Check and (2) I had to pay $270.15

insurance to cover the cost of the lost check. Fortunately I had enough money in my checking account from Daddy's Estate to cover both of the $13,507.65 checks as the first check had not been re-deposited into my account when I had to write the second one. The first check was never found.

Thank goodness the law for passports had been recently changed before I applied for mine to go to Montreal. Before the recent change, Paige, my transgendered sister who went to Montreal for her SRS surgery in January of 2010, said you could not change your gender marker on your passport until after the surgery. That meant when going over to Canada and returning home to the U.S.A., you had to explain to everyone why your passport had a male name, picture, and gender marker. Now the law allows you to apply for a new passport with a female picture and female gender marker if the application includes a letter from your endocrinologist stating you are on hormones and transitioning to female. I got Dr. Obi to draft the letter, included it with my application, proof of name change, female passport pictures, and $100. Within 4 weeks I had my new passport with the correct name, picture, and gender marker. The final piece was now in place for SRS surgery.

I have a dear transgendered sister, Donna, who lives in Iowa. She was having her SRS surgery in October 2010 in Trinidad, Colorado by Dr. Marci Bowers, a highly respected surgeon for SRS. She asked me to come and be with her during the surgery since her family had rejected her. I agreed and flew with her to Trinidad. She had her surgery October 5 and came through with flying colors. Seeing how she recovered from the surgery and the post-surgery health procedures that were needed, helped me tremendously to prepare for my upcoming surgery. I was deeply honored that she asked me to be there with her during this most important time in her life. The bond that formed from this time together will be with both of us the rest of our lives.

All that was left now was to get a pre-surgery physical and a background EKG.

I went to my general physician for my pre-surgery physical and it showed no problems that would prevent me from having SRS. Now I had to go have a background EKG.

Since I hadn't seen my cardiologist in 7 years and I didn't know where he was (he was a member of the Sanger Clinic which was no longer in my hometown), I went to a new cardiologist and told him I needed a background EKG for my Sex Reassignment Surgery. He ran the EKG and it was fine. But he said he also wanted to run a stress test. I agreed and they found my previously diagnosed thoracic aneurysm. I did not tell him of my thoracic aneurysm from 2003 because my earlier cardiologist from Sanger Clinic ran three CT scans over 1.5 years after they found it and they determined the diameter of my aorta didn't change over that time period (i.e. it never changed, remaining 4 cm.). He told me there was no reason for concern as it was only a problem if the wall kept getting thinner as that would increase the potential of it rupturing.

The scans over the 1.5 years showed that was not the case with my aorta. They determined that I was born with the thin wall. He asked me if I had any more CT scans and I told him I had not since my cardiologist said it wasn't necessary. Because of my previous cardiologist's prognosis, I didn't feel it was necessary to tell the new cardiologist of the condition. He was very angry with me when he found out I didn't tell him and threatened to not let me go through with the SRS surgery. He said he was afraid I would die on the operating table from a ruptured aorta. I told him I knew myself pretty well and that I was fine. I told him if I didn't have the surgery I would die anyway from suicide so I might as well have the surgery. Besides, I told him that I couldn't cancel the surgery now without losing all the money I had paid which was $25,000. The thought of not having my SRS got me very upset and my heart started hurting. I told him I was going to have a heart attack right there if he didn't back off. I also told him if I cancelled the surgery, he would have to pay for it as I didn't have another $25,000 to reschedule. He finally backed off. I promised him I would have another CT scan run when I came back from the surgery. He agreed to send the background EKG, stress test results, and blood tests to Dr. Brassard. I checked with Dr. Brassard a week later and he said he received them and all was set for my SRS surgery on January 11, 2011.

My church has been, and always will be, the strength of my life. The church I am a member of, Metropolitan Community Church of Charlotte, is a wonderful, loving church. It is entrenched in the Word of God and understands God's love for all people. They love me very much and they didn't want me to go to Montreal for the surgery alone. So one of my dearest sisters in Christ, Felicia, took time off from work and went with me to Montreal. We took separate flights and she arrived on Saturday and I arrived on Sunday before the surgery. She rented a car and stayed at a hotel in town not too far from the hospital. I was taken to a home where the family of the person having surgery usually stayed.

I stayed there on Sunday night as the Recovery House next to the hospital didn't open until Monday morning. The home was very beautiful. It was laid out like a bed and breakfast. The caretaker and her family lived on the first floor and I stayed on the second floor. It had snowed the day before and the building was covered in snow and was beautiful. The second floor was decorated with early colonial furniture and had a very "homey" feeling.

Felicia came to the home and got me after I got checked in and we went shopping together in Montreal. She thought that it would relax me and it did. As a remembrance I bought a beautiful slate gray dress with black leather angled stripes at a dress shop in a mall. When I got back to the home the caretaker served me dinner in her first floor dining room on Sunday night which was very nice. We talked about my upcoming surgery and she was very supportive and put me at ease. I didn't sleep much that night as I had to take a diuretic to clean my insides out before surgery the next day.

The next morning the caretaker called a cab and he took me to the hospital, Centre Metropolitan de Chirurgie, around 7am. My surgery was scheduled for 11 am. The hospital was much smaller than I imagined. It specialized in transsexual surgeries therefore it never had a lot of patients at any given time. I checked into my room, got into a hospital gown and waited and waited and waited. Around noon I was starting to get nervous. They were running late and I was antsy to get the show on the road. There was no fear that I would change my mind but I was just anxious to get it done. I had waited my whole life for this. Felicia had one of the nurses take our picture together before the surgery. I didn't look very pretty but one thing that struck me about the picture was the joy in my eyes. There was no question I was happy. Felicia told me later that she asked me about how honeybees found flowers with pollen to get my mind off the delay. I immediately jumped in and gave her a dissertation about it. I was so engrossed in answering her question that the extra wait flew by. Finally around 1 pm they came and took me upstairs. I told her I wanted her to be the first person I saw when I woke up, just as Donna wanted me to be the first person she saw when she woke up from her SRS surgery.

When they got me upstairs they put me in a prep room. They immediately covered me in heated blanket which felt wonderful. Then I thought – oh no — how long am I going to be here before they take me into surgery? Within 30 minutes the surgeon came up to me and introduced himself (actually it was the first time I had seen him in person). He quickly put me at ease. He asked me if I had any last minute questions and I said no. I told him I was ready to finally be complete. He smiled and said they would be ready for me in a few minutes. He was right as they came and got me shortly after he left. When they wheeled me into the surgery room I felt like it was finally going to happen.

Most surgery rooms are colder than ice and this was no exception. I felt the extremely cold hard surgery table as they pulled my sheet onto it. As a scientist, I know they need to keep the surgery room cold to keep it sanitary. But still it was even cold for Montreal! One of the doctors pulled my left arm out to start the IV. He, however, was not skilled in starting IV's as he tried 4 times and finally he gave it over to a nurse who had no trouble (my arm was bruised for weeks from the failed IV attempts by the doctor). The nurse on my right turned my arm over so she could read my arm band and asked me the traditional questions as they were putting the IV in. She asked me,

"Why are you here?" I told her, "To have gender reassignment surgery" (in Canada they call it gender reassignment surgery instead of sex reassignment surgery). She told me this was my last opportunity to change my mind. I told her, "Let's get this show on the road". She smiled and that was the last thing I remember before going under for the surgery.

I remember waking up while I was still on the operating table. I felt heavy pushing in my groin area. There was no pain just heavy pushing. Then I heard them say, "We're done" and they wheeled me to recovery. I don't remember much about recovery and Felicia doesn't know how long I was there. She had to wait in my room. I do remember being wheeled back to my room and seeing Felicia's smile and feeling her touch. Her sacrifice and the impact of her presence during this most important time of my life is beyond words. She stayed with me the rest of day (Tuesday) but had to leave on Wednesday as she had to get back to work (she is a teacher in High School).

The surgery procedure is remarkable for male to female gender reassignment surgery. Dr. Brassard uses the penile skin inversion technique. The following description is taken from Dr. Brassard's handout to M2F patients: "The penile skin is inverted to create the vagina (vaginoplasty). If the penis is too short, excess skin from the scrotum is grafted to give sufficient skin for the vaginoplasty. The clitoris is made from an inverted island of the glans (sensate clitoris). The labia minoras are made with the mucosa from the urethra and penile skin during the same procedure. Twelve to sixteen months after surgery the penile head nerves (now the clitoris) re-enervate and the patient is able to have orgasm.

Interestingly Dr. Brassard told me that in SRS, Male to Female, the prostate is not removed. I asked why and he said that sexual orgasm in a male is connected to the prostate and if it is removed it will not occur even after the penal nerves re-enervate. He also said I needed to continue to be checked regularly for prostate cancer.

I was hard on myself during the recovery time in the hospital as I wanted to heal faster than normal. I couldn't walk the hallways as fast and far as I wanted. I remember Donna made 4 complete circles around the Trinidad hallways after her surgery and I wanted to do as well. I kept pressing myself and when I didn't do as well as I felt I should have, I cried. The staff was wonderful as they kept telling me I was doing great. The only problem was I wanted to do better. Then I started worrying that I had not progressed far enough to go the Recovery Facility. The doctor came in Wednesday and said that I did recover enough so they wheeled me, underground, to the Recovery Facility Thursday after the Tuesday surgery.

The Recovery Facility was phenomenal. All the rooms were on the second floor which provided some difficult moments, especially the first week I was there, in getting up and down the stairs for dinner (there was no elevator as they wanted everyone to get exercise going up and down the stairs). There was an ice machine outside my room on the landing, which was very convenient for filling our ice bags which we had to constantly keep on our surgery site the first week after surgery.

Apparently my cardiologist had scared Dr. Brassard regarding my aneurysm as Dr. Brassard ordered an EKG on each of the three days following my surgery. Nothing bad showed up as I suspected and told my cardiologist before I left for Montreal.

The most difficult part of the surgery was not between my legs. It was my sore butt. Even with a cushion on the chair, I couldn't sit at the dining room table for meals for about 5 days post surgery. I ended up standing to eat my meals.

I made a lot of wonderful friends at the bed and breakfast, the hospital and at the Recovery Facility. Everyone was exceptional and I can't say enough about the wonderful care provided there. It definitely was the best choice for the surgery. I stayed at the recovery facility for 12 days. My dear transgendered sister, Paige came up from NC to fly home with me. When she had her surgery she had to fly home alone and she said it was really hard. She said she wasn't going to let me have to do it so she came up to fly back with me. She wanted to see Dr. Brassard again anyway as it had been a year since her SRS surgery. Her gift of love was deeply appreciated.

While I was at the recovery facility the staff taught me how to dilate. This procedure is one that I must do to keep my new vagina from closing. Since I was born male my body 'sees' the new vagina as a hole it must close. To prevent it from closing I dilate with a series of dilators. These dilators (4 in number) start in size with small and work up to large. The dilation schedule requires a post-op transgendered woman to start dilating with the smallest, second, and third size dilators, (5, 10, 15 minutes respectively) 4X a day at least two hours apart, for the first month. Four times a day was hard as it was hard to do when you worked. To dilate you have to lie down, sanitize the dilators and, of course, have privacy. I ended up having to come home and do it during lunch time. Then the frequency changes each week (down from 4X a day to 3X a day to 2X a day to once a day), increasing size of the dilator while decreasing the number of dilators used and decreasing the number of times done each day. After a year, dilation is only needed once a week with the largest dilator. Transgendered women are required to dilate once a week for 15 minutes each time for the rest of their life. Sexual intercourse during the week is an acceptable substitute for the dilation.

I got home fine. I had two wonderful men at the airport wheel me, in a wheel chair, from one end of the airport to the other, to catch my plane. Paige was right. I needed the help. I would not have been able to catch my flights on time without her help and the help of the men at the airports. Pam told me to call her when I got back home to our airport. I got back to NC early so I called her as soon as I got my baggage. She was on her way and hadn't even gotten to the cell phone lot. She came directly to the airport and was somewhat disappointed I was early as she was going to get there early and hold a helium 'bee balloon' up for me to see when I got home. Instead I had to see it in the car. I told her that was okay. The bee balloon was really cute and I loved the thought but most importantly I loved her.

My new life was now in place – I was now a complete woman: emotionally and physically.

Chapter 11
Finding True Joy

According to Social Security Code, in order to change your name you need a copy of the legal court document that says your name has been changed and approved by the court. I did that in January of 2009 when I legally changed my name from Duane James Flynn to Dawn Jennifer Flynn.

If you are a transsexual, Social Security will not change your gender marker without a notarized letter from the surgeon saying that he performed the SRS and that your gender has been changed. So after I got home and recovered enough to travel, I went to Social Security, with my surgeon's letter proving my sex had been changed from male to female, to get my gender marker changed. When I showed them the letter from my surgeon they were happy to change my gender marker on my Social Security records from male to female.

Getting my new birth certificate was another matter. Each state has different requirements to get a new birth certificate. I went to the internet for Oakland County, Michigan, the place I was born, Pontiac to be exact. I figured I needed to send copies of all the necessary legal documents and a letter requesting them to issue a new birth certificate (along with a money order for $15 to cover the cost of the birth certificate) to Vital Records at the Oakland County Health

Department. The website gave me the address and the cost, so I sent the documents April 12, 2011 along with a certified check for $15, figuring that it was a done deal. Little did I know that this was just the beginning of a long process.

I got a return letter in the mail a couple weeks later with my check stating that (1) all change of birth certificates have to go through the Michigan State Department of Vital Records in Lansing, Michigan and (2) that the notarized letter from my surgeon in Montreal, Canada was not acceptable. I had to send THEIR form to him to fill out and notarize. I called the Michigan State Department of Vital Records in Lansing and asked them how much the new birth certificate would cost. The woman there said $40. I asked her if I could use the returned Money Order from the Oakland County Clerk for $15 and add a second Money Order for the remaining $25. She said yes. All I needed to do was change the name of the payee on the first money order to State of Michigan and initial it. So I sent THEIR form to Dr. Brassard in Montreal with a letter and a $35 certified check to get Michigan's form notarized. In the letter I asked him to fill it out, get it notarized, and return it to me so that I could send everything with my new Birth Certificate request form.

When I received his completed form back I then sent it in a package to the Michigan State Department of Vital Records in Lansing, Michigan with the following letter:

April 11, 2011

My name is Dawn Jennifer Flynn. I was born male as Duane James Flynn. I have had Sex Reassignment Surgery (January 11, 2011) and am now legally a woman.

Please find enclosed the following required documentation to create a new birth certificate for me with the name of Dawn Jennifer Flynn and sex Female.

1. *Application to Correct or Change a Michigan Birth Record.*
2. *Certified Copy of Birth Certificate for Duane James Flynn, my original birth.*
3. *The Order and Certificate of Name Change from State of North Carolina, Filed on January 5, 2010, legally changing my name from Duane James Flynn to Dawn Jennifer Flynn.*
4. *Photocopy (front and back) of my current North Carolina Drivers License showing my name (Dawn Jennifer Flynn) and sex (F).*
5. *Two (2) Western Union Money Orders to cover the cost of a new Birth Certificate. One Money Order is for $15 (originally made out to Oakland County Clerk to cover the cost of a new birth certificate application to Oakland County Vital Records). The woman I spoke with during my phone call to Lansing said I could still use the first Money Order, changing the Payee to State of Michigan and initialing it. The second Money Order is for $25 made out to State of Michigan to cover the remainder of the $40 application fee.*
6. *Original sealed State of Michigan Medical Affidavit from Dr. Brassard, the attending physician who performed the Sex Reassignment Surgery on me in Montreal, Canada.*
7. *Photocopy of Dr. Brassard's Board of Medicine Physician License from the State of Michigan.*

Thank you for taking care of this request and assisting me in my transition to female.

Dawn Jennifer Flynn

I sent the package and within 2 weeks I had my new birth certificate as Dawn Jennifer Flynn. Hooray! That was the last of the major changes I needed to do with my new identity.

I love being a girl! I get great joy in getting up in the morning, looking in the mirror and liking what I see. I am a girly girl and love wearing makeup, dresses, heels, and jewelry. In fact, as of this date, I have 105 pairs of earrings. I have several pairs of earrings to go with every outfit I own. When I decide what I am going to wear, I choose the earrings I want to wear and then choose the outfit to match them. I love shopping and trying on clothes. All of these things that a woman does are a great joy for me.

Many women ask me, "Why would you want to be a girl? You are giving up a position of privilege for one of no privilege?" I know I am but I wouldn't change it for the world. My inner soul is that of a woman and is now happy because I can freely express it without fear of ridicule. Being able to be content within myself, being happy in my own skin, and loving myself for the first time is worth the world.

I now understand that true joy only comes when your mind matches your body and you understand that your creator God loves you and accepts you just as you are. When you understand that, you are content within yourself and only then can you love yourself.

In my life before transitioning, none of those applied. Yes, I lived a good life as a man. Yes, I married (twice) and have two beautiful sons. Yes, I faithfully pastored three churches and was blessed to serve them. Yes, I have a beautiful and loving spouse who I love very much and who devoted her life to me and sacrificed much for me. But I was never totally happy.

All my life I would look in the mirror and cry, dying a little each day because deep down I longed to be a woman. The dying each day took its toll to the point of robbing me of the joy that God had for me. I know in my heart that God wants me to be happy. I also know that we must be who we truly are or we are quenching the Holy Spirit, preventing God from truly using us for His glory. I wanted more than anything to please God. I didn't want to quench the Holy Spirit and I didn't want to separate myself from God by sinning. But after much soul searching, I realized I had to be true to myself and decided to transition, to risk it all. When I did, I truly started to live. The decision to step forward and say, "I must do this for myself" started the healing process.

I heard three things all my life in the church – (1) you must love God above all things; (2) you must surrender yourself to Jesus and commit your life to serving Him; and (3) you must sacrifice yourself for others.

The first and third statements come from the Great Commandment found in Matthew 22:37-38 – "Love the Lord your God with all your heart and with all your soul and with all your mind. This is the first and greatest commandment. And the second is like it: Love your neighbor as yourself" (NIV). The second statement about surrendering yourself to Jesus and committing your life to serving Him is obviously connected to the central theme of the New Testament.

The first two precepts—loving God above all things and surrendering to Jesus—I learned growing up in the church. I believed them and tried my best to do them but the struggle with my gender identity conflicted with them. The church kept saying that any thoughts or actions contrary to your God given sex were a sin and was an abomination to God. I didn't want to sin and hurt God. I loved God. I decided to give my life to Jesus when I was working on my Bachelor's degree in Michigan (believer's baptism). I wanted from the deepest part of my soul to serve God and Jesus. I had tried my best to serve them in all I did from family to church to ministry. Yet I was still empty. This conflict eventually drove me to near suicide because it caused me to feel that I had betrayed my family that I loved, and my God and Savior I loved.

But after my SRS my inner self changed. When I looked in the mirror I matched! My body matched my mind. I still cried but it was for joy not for sadness. I was finally whole. And because I felt whole, I started loving myself for the first time in my life. That act of believing I had value and worth then opened the door for me to truly feel the love of my Creator and Savior.

I came to see that our ability to love others, and God, is directly proportional to our ability to love ourselves. I had never truly loved myself because the church had put a guilt complex on me. Now that was over and I have found true joy in life. I have gone back to church and now I feel God's love in ways I couldn't imagine before.

What matters most now is what's in my heart and that is the knowledge that my God and Savior love me. In the gospel of John, chapter 3, verse 16, John writes "For God so loved the world that he gave his one and only son, that whosoever believes in him shall not perish but have eternal life (NIV)". Since the transition I have come to understand, as my pastor has said from the pulpit, that I am a 'whosoever'. I am someone out of the mainstream in today's society.

I am like the beggar, prostitute, leper, blind, demoniac, thief, tax collector, and other outcasts of Jesus' day. I am an outcast as they were. But Jesus gladly associated with them and loved them. He died for them as well as everyone else. I am a 'whosoever' and I know that Jesus died for me.

In the book of Jeremiah, Chapter 1, verse 5, God tells Jeremiah, "Before I formed you in the womb, I knew you, before you were born I set you apart" (NIV). God and Jesus knew I was going to be transgendered when I was still in my Mom's womb and they set me apart for a special ministry. I have nothing to be ashamed of. I truly now understand that God and Jesus' love is for all humankind. His love is always there. We are the ones who limit it, not him.

As I serve my creator God and Savior, I build on the joy that has welled up in my heart. Now I have come to understand the difference between joy and happiness.

Happiness is elation for the circumstances you find yourself in but when the circumstances change, the elation goes away. Happiness is what we feel when we get a gift, or an unexpected day off from work with pay. But when the gift breaks or is lost or when we have to go back to work, the happiness disappears.

Joy, on the other hand, is different.

It is also elation for the circumstances you find yourself in but when the circumstances change, the elation remains. I have joy in knowing my God and savior Jesus loves me no matter what and there is a place waiting for me in heaven when I die. No matter the circumstances, i.e., a lost job, home, friend, partner, parent, child or anything else, my joy is still there.

Second, joy is the knowledge that you are being held and loved by your Creator and Savior all the time and relishing the opportunities to do things, out of love, for others. The Holy Scripture says in Galatians 6:10, "Therefore, as we have opportunity, let us do good to all people..." (NIV). Think about it. The times when you have been the happiest are those times that you have touched someone with love. That indescribable joy comes because it is God confirming, in you, that you have done well. That is the joy of being in the right place, at the right time, doing the right thing for God.

Pam and I are doing okay. We recognize we are soul mates. We have been married 34 years. During that time we have bonded. Pam told me she didn't want a divorce and asked me if I did. I told her I didn't so we have mutually agreed to stay married even though we are living in separate domiciles. We are still legally married (done when I was a male) and we are okay with that.

I have not gotten any sexual libido back yet since the surgery so I don't know if I am straight or gay. As of this writing, I like both men and women equally so I am probably bisexual. I do love looking at sexy men's butts and I love the feel of cuddling with a woman. Until my libido comes back I am going to enjoy experimenting with both genders. Even though I have some attraction to both, I am leaning more right now toward men.

Even though Pam and I are not sexually attracted to each other, we are still each other's best friend and love being together. I know she loves me and that our love will remain after either one of us finds someone else. I love her so much. I would die for her in an instant and I know she would do the same for me. She respects that I am being true to myself and that allows our relationship to be open and honest. Unfortunately her parents and family don't get it. They are totally unable to see past the outside and have consequently rejected me. They want Pam to stop seeing me, get rid of the house and everything connected with me and to start over. I continue to pray that God, someday, will open their hearts and they will come to understand that as imitator's of Christ we, as Christians, must do the same and love all people.

Since joining my church, my faith has come to a point where I needed to commit myself to Christ as my true self. There were a group of new members at church that wanted to be baptized by immersion in a swimming pool owned by a couple at our church. I went to share in their joy but found myself wanting to be re-baptized as Dawn. We all met there at their home and I was immersed and re-baptized as Dawn Jennifer Flynn on August 14, 2011. As I rose from the water, Rev. Catherine said, "God welcomes you, Dawn, as His new daughter." It was a defining moment in my life. My soul rejoiced as God confirmed, in my spirit, that He loved me and I was His daughter. There were no more questions as to who I was. I was God's creation and my life was His.

Yes, I believe that God had a plan for me all along and now I know that His plan required that I must go on this journey. I know in my heart that His plan included every experience that I have had in life to prepare me for this new calling. My journey from my birth until now has been to prepare me for the calling God has had on my life from the beginning. That calling is to share my story with the world and let everyone know that God loves them. Yes, His love is not confined to only those who fit into society's definition of desirable and lovable. It is for all.

Yes, I am a sinful creature. But contrary to what the church implied, being transgendered was not living in sin and has not separated me from God. **I know in my heart that God does love me! Hallelujah!** And yes, He loves you too, for we all are His divine creation.

Acknowledgements

No book is a product of its own. It is the product of the writer, those who have had input into the information in the book, and those who have made its publication possible. This book is no exception therefore I would like to acknowledge those who have had a part in my life experiences that are not mentioned in the body of the book and have had a part in its successful publication. There were many people who I have known through the years that have had tremendous influence in making me who I am today.

The influence of my pastor, Rev. Catherine Houchins, cannot be overstated. When my faith and belief in God was shattered she was there supporting, encouraging and believing in me all of which was instrumental in helping get back in touch with my faith and my calling.

The support and love of my entire church family at Metropolitan Community Church of Charlotte, NC is my spiritual mainstay. They have accepted me totally and unconditionally from the first day I entered the church's doors. My faith is strengthened every day as I remember their love and the love of Jesus that lives within them. Thank you all for being there for me when I needed you.

To my dearest friends who love me knowing about my journey: Allein, Ann, Debbie and Joal, Denise and Dean, Henry, David G. and Pam, Alan and Ann, Pacilla, Jim C. and Cherie, Hugh, Steve, Annette, Rich, Cecil, Bob, Jim B., Jane, Kelly, Christina, Lorrie. Suzie (her children Dori and John), Donna, David and Libby, Ken and Laverne, Jann, Jim H., Kate, Libby, Missy, Vicki and Jimmy, Tricia and Michael, Dierdre and Alan, Wendy, Lauren, Jenny, Sherrie, Maria, Stacy, Heather, Liz, Jasmin, Star, Kay, Nancy, Bernice, Doug, Lou Ann, Hunter, Karen, Sharon, and my trans family especially Charles and Johnny, David and Debbie, Paula, and Gina.

To Frank, Felicia "Chicago", Tia, and Felicia, thank you for your manuscript review and comments, along with making it possible to put my story into print. This book is a testament to your sacrifice and love.

To all of these, I say thank you so much for being a large part of my life. My prayer is that this book shows you that your life has made a difference and I thank God for all of you.

About The Author
Dawn J. Flynn

Before the author transitioned, she graduated with honors from High School (1967), B.A. cum laude (1971), M.S. in Entomology (1974). Did PhD work at Michigan State in insect taxonomy (1975-1980).

Honors include Hubert Lyman Clark Award for outstanding original science research (1971), Alpha Chi and Sigma Zeta National Science Honorary (1971), Sigma Xi Research Honorary (1974), Myers Memorial United Methodist Man of the Year (1987), elected to Marqui Who's Who (2002, 2003), and Continental Who's Who (2009).

Activity in the community has included the Board of Directors for Gaston County Humane Society (1985-1989), President of Gaston Audubon Society (1989), Representative on Audubon Council of North Carolina (1987-1994) and Treasurer (1988-1994), Water

Quality Chairman of Gaston County Quality of Natural Resources Committee (1993-1995), Founder and First President of Gaston County Birding Club (2002).

Before transition she received a Course of Study Certificate (M.Div. equivalent) from Duke Seminary (2002), and served as pastor to three Methodist churches in North Carolina from 1997-2008, elected to Heritage Who's Who (2010).

Professional accomplishments include numerous pamphlets, brochures, a training manual in entomology and articles on treehoppers of North Carolina and Panama. Professionally she is a member of Entomological Society of America, Entomological Society of Washington (DC) and Coleopterist Society.

In addition to her professional publishing and activities, Dawn, is also the Minister of Congregational Care in her Charlotte MCC church and an activist for transgender rights, telling her story in public forums to encourage those on their journey and to educate any and all on God's love for all people. She is currently employed as an entomologist ("the Bug Lady") at the Schiele Museum and is living in Gastonia, NC.

Made in the USA
Columbia, SC
23 August 2021